Academic Libraries:
The Changing Knowledge Centers of Colleges and Universities

by Barbara B. Moran

ASHE-ERIC Higher Education Research Report No. 8, 1984

Prepared by

 ®Clearinghouse on Higher Education
The George Washington University

Published by

Association for the Study of Higher Education

Jonathan D. Fife,
Series Editor

Cite as:
Moran, Barbara B. *Academic Libraries: The Changing Knowledge Centers of Colleges and Universities.* ASHE-ERIC Higher Education Research Report No. 8. Washington, D.C.: Association for the Study of Higher Education, 1984.

The ERIC Clearinghouse on Higher Education invites individuals to submit proposals for writing monographs for the Higher Education Research Report series. Proposals must include:
1. A detailed manuscript proposal of not more than five pages.
2. A 75-word summary to be used by several review committees for the initial screening and rating of each proposal.
3. A vita.
4. A writing sample.

Library of Congress Catalog Card Number: 85-61910
ISSN 0737-1292
ISBN 0-913317-17-9

ERIC° Clearinghouse on Higher Education
The George Washington University
One Dupont Circle, Suite 630
Washington, D.C. 20036

ASHE Association for the Study of Higher Education
One Dupont Circle, Suite 630
Washington, D.C. 20036

This publication was partially prepared with funding from the National Institute of Education, U.S. Department of Education, under contract no. 400-82-0011. The opinions expressed in this report do not necessarily reflect the positions or policies of NIE or the Department.

EXECUTIVE SUMMARY

The libraries of America's colleges and universities are in the midst of a period of unprecedented change and adjustment. Academic libraries have never been static organizations; they have existed within and responded to changes in the institutions of higher education they serve. The typical academic library has grown from a one-room affair open only a few hours a week to a complex organization employing a large staff and housing hundreds of thousands of volumes.

Today's academic libraries are facing a series of challenges that arise from factors both internal and external to the library itself. As libraries, the primary information resources on campuses, enter the so-called "information age," they face a number of common problems. Libraries' responses to these challenges will determine the shape of the academic library of the future.

What Effect Will New Technology Have on Academic Libraries?

New technological developments have already profoundly affected academic libraries. Almost every function carried out in a library has been altered to some extent by advances in electronics, computerization, and telecommunications. At one time, for example, each library largely did its own cataloging. In 1971, the first online shared cataloging system was established. More of these bibliographic utilities have since been established, and now most cataloging in academic libraries is produced through the shared cataloging database of one of these utilities. Services for users have been greatly expanded by the use of online bibliographic search services, which became common in the 1970s. Instead of manually searching indexes to find citations or produce bibliographies, a trained searcher can manipulate a computer database that produces the same results in a matter of minutes. Interlibrary loan, library acquisitions, and circulation have all benefited from the use of computerized systems. Many academic libraries now have electronic antitheft devices to retard unauthorized "borrowing" from the collection. Photocopying machines have changed library users' note-taking patterns in less than a generation.

These developments, immense as they have been, are merely forerunners of the technologies that will be common in libraries of the future. Some libraries have already introduced online public access catalogs to replace traditional card catalogs. Some libraries are using new methods of information storage, such as digitally encoded video discs. Future interlibrary loans will bypass the postal system and use new methods, such as digital telefacsimile, for document delivery.

Libraries will indeed live in a "brave new world," but they will find technology very expensive. Despite earlier hopes that automation might lead to reduced costs, such reductions have yet to be realized.

> *Technology provides us with many options, only some of which we can afford. But we must recognize clearly that in applying technology to the service of scholarship, in some areas we have no choice. We are not replacing traditional services because we prefer the new gadgetry but because we no longer have the resources necessary to make the old ways effective in the current environment* (Battin 1982a, pp. 581–82).

How Can Libraries Meet the Rising Cost of Materials?

The acquisition budgets of academic libraries in the 1970s were not able to keep pace with the soaring prices of library materials. Prices for both books and journals ran far ahead of general inflation. The serious erosion of the buying power of the library's acquisition budget occurred at the same time that financial problems became severe throughout all of higher education. Thus, colleges and universities were unable to provide sufficient funds for library budgets to keep pace with inflation. At the same time, the output from publishers increased dramatically, with the result that libraries added a smaller percentage of the published literature to their collections.

Academic libraries, even those that pride themselves on their extensive collections, have reluctantly realized that they can no longer acquire and house comprehensive book collections. The consensus is that no library, however large, can afford to achieve self-sufficiency; thus, networks must be established to permit the cooperative sharing of library resources. The time has come to accelerate "the trend away from each library being a self-contained unit, toward a system in which the library will be a service center, capable of linking users to national bibliographic files and distant collections" (National Enquiry 1979, p. 159). Many library users, who would prefer to see their libraries continue to purchase the bulk of the scholarly materials they need, will likely resist this new emphasis on access rather than acquisition. Nonetheless, it is inevitable that collection development policies, especially in large libraries, will respond to new economic realities. The formation of consortia and the development of a national cooperative strategy promise continued access by scholars to the world's literature at a less burdensome cost.

What Is the Appropriate Role for Librarians?

The library is a highly labor-intensive organization; thus, issues relating to staffing and personnel are critical. Development of new staffing patterns has resulted in many tasks previously handled by professional librarians being turned over to students, clerks, or paraprofessionals. The new technological developments require more sophisticated librarians, and the role of the academic librarian is being reinterpreted to provide more effective service to library users. Reflecting this new professionalism is the renewed emphasis on instruction in library and information skills. Librarians now take an active responsibility for facilitating students' and faculty's use of the library's resources.

A closely related issue is that of status for the librarian: Should the academic librarian have the same status as the faculty and be governed by the same or similar standards for promotion and tenure, or is another status more appropriate? After a strong push for faculty status in the 1960s, some librarians are reversing their stand on the issue, and a lively debate has ensued. Another issue, the type of education and background most appropriate for librarians planning to enter academic libraries, is still to be resolved.

How Should Libraries Be Managed?

The problems academic libraries face in the area of management stem in part from the fact that budget support depends upon justifying services and programs to students, faculty, and administrators. Although the library usually is one of the largest cost centers on the campus, it has few ways to generate funds for its support (Galvin and Lynch 1982, p. 1). The costly effects of inflation, the growth in the volume of publication, and the implementation of expensive new technologies have caused some academic administrators to view the library as a "bottomless pit" capable of absorbing all the funds appropriated to it and always needing more. The increasing complexity of the library organization and budgetary pressures have forced academic librarians to pay increasing attention to administrative matters. Although many libraries are still governed in a hierarchical manner, employees' involvement in governance has become of interest. In some libraries tension has arisen between the desire of the staff to have greater participation in decision making and the library director's accountability for the library's administration. In other institutions the advent of collective bargaining and faculty status for librarians has further complicated governance. The more successful libraries will likely implement governance plans that allow professional librarians a meaningful role in the library's policy decisions but spell out administrative responsibility in detail.

How Can Existing Collections in Academic Libraries Be Preserved?

Librarians have always assumed that preservation of recorded knowledge is one of their central functions, but today's academic libraries face an intractable preservation problem. Improper storage facilities, the overuse or misuse of collections, and the use of acids in paper manufactured during the past 100 years have resulted in the physical deterioration of a large and growing part of this country's library collections. Regardless of cause, an alarming percentage of collections need procedures implemented to preserve the existing stock. Although techniques are now available to aid in preserving and restoring library collections, successful preservation presents a challenge to both librarians and scholars. Priorities need to be set and a national plan implemented to ensure that the content of millions of published materials will not be lost. As with technology, the cost is likely to be high.

What Will the Academic Library of Tomorrow Look Like?

Over the next one or two decades, academic libraries will change. Some have predicted the virtual disappearance of libraries as electronic communication leads to a paperless society, but more likely libraries of the future will neither disappear nor become paperless, because the vast retrospective collections they hold are available nowhere else. Books and computer output will coexist. Users will still go to libraries to find collections of materials that are not available elsewhere or that they cannot afford (De Gennaro 1982).

New technologies and economic constraints will continue to reshape academic libraries. Academic administrators should not underestimate the severity of the problems that will confront college and university libraries during this period. The higher education community needs to reassess its traditional concept of academic libraries and join with librarians to develop a consensus about the appropriate role and mission of the academic library of the future.

CONTENTS

CONTENTS

FOREWORD

Second to the faculty, the most important source of knowledge on a college campus is the academic library. Yet this vital asset is more often than not taken for granted, with little effort made by administrators to understand its exact fit within the institution or to recognize that its future may also be the institution's future. Today's academic libraries and their staffs are caught in the middle of the information revolution, between traditional academic conservatism and tantalizing possibilities of the high-tech world.

As the result of burgeoning new technologies (online systems, video discs, and microphotography) and a change in philosophy toward shared resources, campus libraries are facing a new frontier. The frontier holds much promise, but it also has grave implications for budgets and management that must be carefully addressed.

In this Research Report, Barbara B. Moran, assistant professor at the School of Library Science, University of North Carolina at Chapel Hill, carefully reviews and synthesizes more than 180 publications that examine academic libraries. This vast amount of material is organized into four areas significant to college and university administrators: the impact of new technology, management, personnel issues, and library collections and cooperation. This definitive review of academic libraries greatly helps clarify their status, their potential, and the problems that need to be addressed, and it should help administrators face the issues, acknowledge that academic libraries are integral to institutional vitality, and plug their colleges into the information age.

Jonathan D. Fife
Series Editor
Professor and Director
ERIC Clearinghouse on Higher Education
The George Washington University

ACKNOWLEDGMENTS

I would like to acknowledge the help of Jonathan Fife, Series Editor, and the staff of the ERIC Clearinghouse on Higher Education for their help in preparing this monograph.

I am indebted to my colleagues, Mildred Downing, Judith Wood, and Joe Hewitt, who provided me with valuable information and assistance. I especially appreciate the help of Edward G. Holley, who read the manuscript and provided both critical comments and encouragement.

My graduate assistant, Elizabeth Wagner, assembled material for the bibliography and helped to trace down elusive sources. The task of completing the monograph would have been much more difficult without her. I am grateful to Jackie Girardeau for her help in typing and retyping the manuscript.

Finally, I am indebted to my husband, Joe, and my sons, Michael and Brian, for all their help and encouragement.

INTRODUCTION

Academic libraries have been a part of American higher education since its beginning. A letter written in 1638 confirms the presence of a library at what would become Harvard College: "Newtowne now is called Cambridge. There is a University house reared, I heare, and a prity library begun" (quoted in Hamlin 1981, p. 4). The "prity" library consisted of books donated by local residents. It was enlarged the next year, when John Harvard's will left one-half of his estate to be used for establishing a college and all of his library, 329 titles in more than 400 volumes. Other books were added so that by 1655, the library at Harvard had grown to approximately 900 volumes (Hamlin 1981, p. 4).

The academic libraries of the colonial period and up to the last half of the nineteenth century offered little to either faculty or students. They were usually small collections, open only a few hours a week, with restrictive conditions and policies severely limiting physical access to the books.

Libraries gained greater prominence during the period of university growth following the Civil War. With the founding of Johns Hopkins in 1876, a new emphasis was placed on research, new curricula emphasized electives, and the seminar system required an expansion of academic libraries. Growth in resources was one of the major trends in academic libraries during the late nineteenth and early twentieth centuries. Acquisition of all types of materials—including a large number of journals—was crucial if the library was to support research (Edelman and Tatum 1976, p. 224). Library acquisitions grew rapidly, and the quality of the library came to be defined almost exclusively in terms of its holdings. Except for Harvard, no academic library claimed more than 100,000 volumes in 1876, but by 1920 many libraries exceeded that number (Shiflett 1981, p. 126).

The growth of collections was accompanied by a number of other changes in academic libraries of the time. Full-time librarians began to be employed. Hours were extended and the physical facilities improved to provide students and faculty with more comfortable working conditions. Parent institutions assumed the responsibility for regularly financing the library to provide staff and to guarantee acquisitions of books and journals (Hamlin 1981, p. 49). By the early twentieth century, libraries were increasingly recognized as essential to the academic enterprise. The phrase "heart of the university" came into vogue to describe the integral role libraries played in higher education.

By the early twentieth century, libraries were increasingly recognized as essential to the academic enterprise.

A period of unparalleled growth began for academic libraries with the expansion of higher education after World War II, and it continued throughout the 1960s. Library collections grew at a phenomenal rate. In 1972, for example, Cornell University noted that it had taken 70 years to acquire its first million books, 20 years for the second, nine years for the third, and six years for the fourth (Kaser 1980, p. 47). Many universities and colleges built new library buildings, and everywhere the size of the staff and the size of the budget multiplied. But all was not well.

During the last two decades academic libraries in parallel with their parent institutions experienced the greatest period of growth and affluence that they have ever known. The watchword was "more"—more money, more books and staff, more space, and more technology. . . . Although libraries got more of everything during those years, they still could not keep pace with the growth of new fields of research, new doctoral programs, and the increased production of books and journals. Two decades of affluence not only failed to help solve the many problems that were brought on by exponential growth—they exacerbated them (De Gennaro 1975, p. 917).

This period of expansion was followed by the "new depression" in higher education. The tight budgets of the 1970s and 1980s took their toll on libraries, both in collections and in staffs. Still, the growth in research and publication continued unabated.

Today's academic libraries stand at a crossroads. They must move beyond, as indeed many already have, their traditional role as custodians of books and integrate new methods of storage and transmission of information into an already existing organization. They must, at the same time, absorb the pervasive changes that new technology will make on the organization.

University libraries are being pummelled by profound and undoubtedly permanent changes. For example, the distinction between public and technical services appears to be eroding; communications within the library and outside organizations are taking on a new dimension; and new demands are being placed on professional staff. These shifts and turns, moreover, are not one-time modifications to

*which libraries subsequently adjust, quickly rebounding to
the status quo. Rather automation apparently introduces
continuous change; relentless revision is now inexorably an
attribute of the university library* (Cline and Sinnott 1983,
p. 172).

This monograph describes contemporary academic libraries
and discusses the central issues and problems as they move
into the information age. The amount of literature relating to
academic libraries is vast, and the monograph does not pre-
tend to serve as a comprehensive review of the literature on
academic libraries or as a complete examination of every
aspect of academic librarianship.

Because the libraries in community colleges differ greatly
from their counterparts in four-year colleges and universities,
the monograph makes no attempt to discuss community college libraries. It does examine the libraries of four-year colleges and major universities, but the emphasis is on large
university libraries. Although small and medium-sized libraries
vastly outnumber large research libraries, the latter type is
treated more thoroughly, not only because more has been published about university libraries but also because the changes
now taking place in academic libraries are more apparent in
them. The size of research libraries forced them to adopt
technological changes early. The use of new technology will
likely flow down from the larger institutions to the smaller;
thus, the shape of the academic library of the future can be
more clearly discerned by studying large libraries. Where
they lead, smaller libraries will probably follow, at least to
the extent that their users and their collections can benefit
from the innovations.

ACADEMIC LIBRARIES AND THE NEW TECHNOLOGIES

Libraries are at a critical point in their history. They have tremendous investments in their existing collections, catalog card files, and manual procedures. But society will not wait for libraries to accommodate themselves gradually to the changing world of computer technology. The "Information Age" is here to stay, and libraries must join the mainstream of progress or find themselves slowly eddying around in a backwash of antiquated products and services (Fayen 1983, p. 1).

Libraries of all types are in the middle of what has been called a "quiet revolution." "It is quiet because the signs of change are subtle and not always evident. It is a revolution because the new technology will most surely affect all libraries" (Becker 1978, p. 413). Today's libraries are in transition from manual to electronic systems. The computer has already greatly affected libraries and promises to increase that effect in the future. Databases are replacing card catalogs and printed indexes and abstracts. Information is being produced and stored in new forms. The merger of computers and printing is leading to a new method of information transfer. Libraries are no longer self-sufficient but are linked through electronic networks of various types. The changes brought about by advances in technology have been so extensive that it is difficult to assess their total effect, but it is clear that libraries are in a stage of fundamental transformation. Libraries are being "reinvented in the electronic environment" (Battin 1984, p. 170).

Libraries cannot shut down while they are being reinvented, however, so librarians face the task of integrating the new technology into an already existing organization while attempting to maintain most of its traditional features. Their task is further complicated by the fact that the types of technologies found in present-day libraries vary widely. New technologies rarely completely replace the previous ones (Atkinson 1984). Libraries exhibit this mix of technologies perhaps more clearly than any other institution. The diversification is exemplified in the library's potential holdings, which may range from clay tablets and papyrus to digitized video discs and electronic databases. In terms of processing and handling these materials, librarians also rely on a variety of technologies from pencils to computer terminals. New technologies have always existed alongside the old ones. What is different about the present era is the rapid pace of the development, where change must be dealt with continuously.

The use of the new technologies is changing not only the type of materials libraries collect but how these materials are processed and handled.

The famous line from Thomas Carlyle, "The true university is a collection of books," may have been true in his day, but it is not true today.... Universities and the libraries that serve them must be much more than collections of books.... The way libraries are operated and funded must change if they are to continue to fulfill their mission of supporting instruction and research in this rapidly changing environment (De Gennaro 1984b, p. 1205).

Academic libraries must search for a way to superimpose modern information services upon their traditional functions while they make the transition into the information age. By the end of this century, most libraries will have made the transition and will be fulfilling their traditional mission differently with the help of new technology.

Libraries have already been changed immensely by automation, although other factors have also led to changes. If none of the new technologies had ever been introduced into academic libraries, today's library would doubtlessly be different from the library of the past. Academic libraries would have changed in response to shifts in institutions of higher education—in response to factors like the development of new disciplines, the influx of different types of students, and altering patterns of financial support. Nonetheless, sometime in the future when library historians look back upon the period from the late 1960s through the 1990s, it is likely that they will see the introduction of the new technologies as the driving force behind most of the changes in academic libraries during that era. The changes brought about by their introduction have been so pervasive that the theme of technological innovation runs like a thread throughout this entire monograph. This section examines some of the specific changes that have occurred in academic libraries because of the introduction of new technologies and discusses the likely impact of technology in the future.

Computers and Libraries
Computers are such an integral part of modern society that it is easy to forget how recent their development has been. Although the first computer was built just before World

War II, general-purpose computers were not common before about 1960.

Widespread interest in the application of computers in libraries grew during the 1960s. Computers seemed to provide an ideal mechanism for dealing with a particular problem in library operations:

> *The operation of a university library is driven by data—its creation and storage, retrieval and review, modification and manipulation. Indeed, librarians spend considerably more time processing information about books and serials than they devote to handling the objects themselves* (Cline and Sinnott 1983, pp. 12–13).

Librarians were eager to adopt computer automation to help support data processing. The unprecedented growth in demand for the services of academic libraries and in the growth of their collections during the 1960s were added to incentives to investigate the possibility of using computers to perform routine library operations. The manual systems employed by librarians at that time had reached and often exceeded the limits of their effectiveness.

Libraries thus began to automate some of their functions during the early 1960s. The National Library of Medicine, the University of California at San Diego, and Southern Illinois University were all pioneers in library automation (Salmon 1975, p. 4). The Intrex project (Information Transfer Experiments) at MIT, the first large-scale experiment in library automation, began in 1965, as did the MARC (Machine Readable Cataloging) project at the Library of Congress. MARC was initiated to define a format for machine-readable catalog cards that could be used interchangeably on many different types of computers (Salmon 1975, p. 5). Because most universities did not have access to time-sharing systems until the late 1960s, nearly all of the early systems were batch oriented. All of these systems required the use of a main-frame computer, and most of them were designed to automate the record-keeping or "housekeeping" functions of librarianship: acquisitions, circulation, and cataloging.

Interest in library automation grew in the 1970s despite the general decline in funding in higher education and academic libraries. Many of the advances in automation during that decade were the result of the entrance of the commercial sector into the library automation market (Cline and Sinnott

1983, p. 14). The commercial firms had sold individual libraries hardware and expertise during the 1960s, but during the 1970s vendors began to market complete packaged systems (so-called "turnkey" systems) that libraries could install and use immediately because a single vendor supplied all hardware, software, installation, training, and continuing support for the system. In 1974, one vendor marketed such systems; by 1979 there were nine (Boss 1984). Commercial firms also provided a type of computer system that brought the retrieval capabilities of automation directly to the library user. Major commercial vendors such as Lockheed Information Systems, Systems Development Corporation (SDC), and Bibliographic Retrieval Services (BRS) began to market online search systems that permitted the exploration of databases to answer reference questions or to provide computer-generated bibliographies for users.

By the 1980s, many academic libraries had made great progress in using computer technology to keep records and to assist patrons in their use of the library's materials. As would be expected, the large academic libraries had done the most with the automation, but almost all academic libraries, no matter how small, were using specific automated processes like, for instance, one of the online shared cataloging databases. A few libraries developed integrated automated systems in which a single bibliographic file supported a variety of library functions, such as acquisitions, serials, cataloging, and circulation. These integrated systems had the advantage of needing only one input or update to keep the entire database current for all functions. Although a few integrated systems exist and others are being planned, most libraries "rejected the integrated approach in favor of automating only those functions that appear to lend themselves to rapid and less expensive automation" (Boss 1984, p. 1183). In those libraries, automation was implemented by the evolutionary process of incorporating discrete computerized systems into their operations. Circulation, serials control, and acquisitions were functions frequently automated first.

Three developments seem to have had the widest impact on the overall effects of automation in academic libraries: the growth and development of bibliographic utilities, the changes brought about in information retrieval by the use of online databases, and the more recent development of online public access catalogs.

Bibliographic Utilities

Bibliographic utilities have grown and thrived chiefly because of the assistance they provide in cataloging. Because of their influence, cataloging has been perhaps the area of librarianship most revolutionized by the use of automation.

Librarians realized long ago that merely collecting books was not enough: Cataloging was necessary to give information about and to provide physical and intellectual access to library collections. Cataloging includes the tasks of recording, describing, and indexing the items in a library's collection, and it is generally considered to consist of two components. The first is descriptive cataloging, which describes the item as an object in terms of author, title, publisher, date of publication, size, and number of pages. The second is subject cataloging, which is concerned with the content of the item and involves two processes: classification according to a standardized system in which the work is given a "call number" and the assignment of subject headings that allow multiple access to the work.

Descriptive and subject cataloging can be a time-consuming task. The Library of Congress has estimated that its catalogers need from three to five hours to catalog a typical book (Goodwin 1974, p. 90). The intellectual task of describing the physical item and analyzing its subject content has been little changed by automation, but computers have been used to perform the clerical processes involved, to produce a wide variety of products from the cataloging record, and to promote the sharing of cataloging records among many libraries. This last function is most important because if cataloging records can be shared so that each library does not have to catalog individually each item for the first time, the costs of cataloging can be drastically reduced.

In this country, the Library of Congress has always been the largest provider of shared cataloging records; it has sold copies of its printed catalog cards to other libraries since 1901. The MARC project, begun in 1965, is widely accepted as the most significant development in the history of library automation (Salmon 1975, p. 85). The project was designed to enable the Library of Congress to make its cataloging data available in machine-readable form, which could be used for many purposes. The Library of Congress used it to automate its card-production division, which supplies millions of printed cards each year to libraries around the world. Other libraries used the machine-readable tapes to produce book catalogs in hard copy or in microform. (These microform catalogs are generally known as COM [computer output microform] catalogs.) The MARC tapes also represented a giant step forward in shared cataloging, because they constitute a major portion of the shared cataloging records that are stored and provided to member libraries by the cataloging networks or bibliographic utilities. Because few libraries could afford the large computer systems required for storing and handling the MARC tapes, the bibliographic utilities provided access to machine-readable cataloging records without the need for enormous investments in automation by individual institutions.

The oldest and largest of these bibliographic utilities is OCLC (an acronym that first stood for Ohio College Library Center but now stands for Online Computer Library Center). OCLC began in 1968 as a statewide consortium of college and university libraries in Ohio. It brought up the first online shared cataloging system in 1971. Members of OCLC found they were able to use the OCLC database to improve the speed and efficiency of their cataloging. When an item entered the individual library and needed to be cataloged, instead of performing original cataloging or ordering the catalog cards from the Library of Congress, a searcher could search the OCLC database by entering short strings of certain characters into the library's OCLC terminal. To search by author, for example, the searcher enters the first three characters of the author's last name, the first two characters of the first name, and the middle initial. Cataloging records of all works by that author contained in the database can then be displayed on the screen. The searcher can accept the cataloging record as displayed and order cards or can enter modifications to adapt that record to the local library's cataloging practice and then order cards that will incorporate those modifications. If the searcher does not find an already existing record for the item, a cataloger might catalog that item and then enter that catalog record into the shared database for the use of other members of the bibliographic utility.

The OCLC system provided a method for libraries to significantly reduce the large costs associated with original cataloging. Because both the MARC records prepared by the Library of Congress and the cataloging records provided by all other member libraries can be accessed and used, no library except the first to obtain a specific item would have to produce an original record. Professional catalogers could be replaced by paraprofessionals who would locate, verify, and accept cataloging copy provided online. OCLC greatly affected the workflow and productivity of cataloging departments and often spurred a reexamination of the organization of the cataloging department itself (Gapen 1979).

Libraries outside Ohio quickly recognized the advantages of OCLC and wanted access to the same type of system. A number of existing and newly formed regional consortia at first planned to replicate the OCLC system, but after OCLC proved willing to provide its services to the other libraries, the regional networks decided not to replicate but instead to serve as regional service centers that would broker OCLC services to member libraries (De Gennaro 1979). By 1984, over 4,800 libraries belonged to OCLC. Its database as of December 1984 contained nearly 11.5 million bibliographic records and was growing by about 23,000 bibliographic records weekly (OCLC 1984). OCLC now has revenues of more than $47 million a year and the largest research and development staff in librarianship (Boss 1984, p. 1184).

Although OCLC is the largest, it is not the only bibliographic utility. The Research Libraries Group (RLG), a group of large research universities and their libraries, offers a shared bibliographic service, RLIN, that provides online access to the holdings of its member libraries. RLIN offers some unique features, including its computerized capacity to achieve bibliographic control of East Asian vernacular material. Unlike OCLC, which attempts to meet the varied needs of many types of libraries, RLIN is designed to meet the specific needs of large research libraries. A third major bibliographic cooperative operates in the United States, but its scope is regional rather than national: The Washington Library Network (WLN) serves mostly libraries in the northwest. UTLAS, a Canadian bibliographic utility, also has some members in the United States.

Most academic libraries are now members of one of the bibliographic utilities. Although use of these utilities has reduced the time and expense associated with original cataloging, the cost of membership in such an organization is now a large item in a library's budget. The cost varies greatly from library to library, depending on the utility and the amount and type of services used. As one example, the Academic Affairs Library at the University of North Carolina at Chapel Hill estimates its total institutional cost for membership in OCLC and in SOLINET, its regional network, to be nearly $135,000 for fiscal year 1983–84. This figure includes not only membership fees but also charges for telecommunication, terminal maintenance, and transactions.*

Although originally used primarily to allow libraries to reduce the costs of cataloging, the bibliographic utilities have proved invaluable to academic libraries for other purposes as well. One of their other major functions is to serve as a network for sharing resources. When a user needs a specific work that the library does not own, the library can use the online search capabilities of the utilities to find out what other library owns the needed item. The increased access to resources at other libraries permits a library to spend its acquisition budget on the material most needed by its users and to rely on other libraries for lesser used materials.

The bibliographic utilities have also permitted individual libraries to share the benefits of sophisticated technology without having to bear the full cost of the development and operation of this technology. The bibliographic utilities are "change agents" for libraries because they provide three critical services: research and development, capital acquisition, and mechanisms for technology transfer (Markuson 1979, p. 125).

Despite similarities in their basic services, fundamental differences exist between the utilities in terms of specific services offered, the cataloging standards imposed by the utility, and the ease with which files can be browsed (Cline and Sinnott 1983, p. 17). All of them, however, have gone beyond being merely a cataloging database and now provide various systems that aid in acquisitions, interlibrary loan, serials control, and the conversion of old catalog cards into machine-readable form. As yet the various networks are not linked; which sometimes creates problems of access for scholars because a library usually participates in only one network (Battin 1984, p. 173). Others argue, however, that a national bibliographic network would be too expensive and too cumbersome and would be useful only to the nation's largest research libraries (Malinconico 1980, p. 1792).

Without a doubt the bibliographic utilities have been one of the success stories of library automation. But even though these utilities have become essential to libraries of all types and sizes, some changes in their structure and functions are

*Joe Hewitt (Associate University Librarian for Technical Services, University of North Carolina at Chapel Hill) 1984, personal communication.

likely during the 1980s. The networks are threatened both by their high costs and by the desire of individual libraries for autonomy in local cataloging standards (Martin 1984, p. 1194). In addition:

Those utilities usually operate on large computers, technology more representative of the 1970s than that of the 1980s. Those systems were designed ten or more years ago, and do not easily adapt to the rapid changes in technology that have characterized the past few years. The large online systems and their associated networks are in danger of becoming "dinosaurs." At a time when it is relatively easy to purchase a personal computer for the home, and even the smallest institution can buy a microcomputer, these "dinosaurs" must move rapidly to prove their value to their clientele, and thus avoid extinction (Martin 1984, p. 1195).

And a move away from the utilities toward some form of distributed network is possible, based on agreements that encourage sharing of information and resources among libraries in specific regions (Beckman 1983, p. 282).

Another problem that might limit the use of bibliographic utilities is possible changes in telecommunication costs brought on by the breakup of AT&T. If costs of long-line distribution turn out to be cheaper than those for local distribution, national or regional centralized information such as is provided by the bibliographic utilities will continue to be used. If, on the other hand, the reverse is true, a shift to decentralization would be likely (Atkinson 1984, p. 59). Libraries would rely more on shared cataloging distributed among a group of local institutions. Although libraries have been examining a number of alternatives to the use of telephones—satellites, fiber optics, and cable television, for example—the prospects for widespread implementation of any of these alternatives in the near future are not bright (Boss 1984, p. 1188).

As automation progresses and libraries continue to develop local, integrated, multifunction systems that can handle a variety of library functions, the role of the utilities might diminish. The development of integrated systems has led a number of libraries to limit the role of their bibliographic utility to that of a supplier of database resources (Boss 1984).

After obtaining a machine-readable record from the utility's database, many libraries do all subsequent searching and editing locally. As interfaces are developed among the local library systems in a region, the use of the utilities' databases for interlibrary loan [ILL] also changes. Already some libraries use the utilities' ILL subsystems only to access out-of-state locations (Boss 1984, p. 1184).

During the 1970s, bibliographic utilities became an integral part of most academic libraries, both large and small. But certain critical issues need to be resolved during the 1980s: their interrelationship, the optimal configuration of hardware and software needed, the library activities that can best be served by the utilities (Cline and Sinnott 1983, p. 19), and the ownership of data in the shared cataloging databases. This issue of ownership is central to future library economics and operations (Avram 1984, p. 67), and OCLC's recent decision to copyright its database could mark a fundamental change in the cooperative agreements. Because they affect so many libraries, the future of these networks is likely to remain a topic of great concern to the library community during this decade.

Online Databases
The bibliographic utilities were used chiefly to allow librarians to catalog material more efficiently, but it was not until the widespread availability of online bibliographic databases during the 1970s that new technology was brought directly to the library's users. The number of commercial databases grew dramatically during the 1970s. The ability to search an online database evolved during the decade from a specialized service for an elite group of researchers to a service available to faculty and students in a large number of academic libraries.

Today individual libraries are linked to the online computers by computer terminals, telephone lines, and data communications networks. Already more than 2,000 databases are available, and the number is increasing at the rate of 20 to 30 percent a year (Williams 1984, p. 1). Librarians use online databases to prepare customized bibliographies, to verify bibliographic citations, and to answer reference questions. A few minutes at a computer terminal can provide information that would have taken hours to compile manually. The availability of online databases has revolutionized the way libraries are able to retrieve information for users.

Many of these databases developed as a by-product of electronic publishing. During the 1960s, as a result of the spiraling growth of journals, publishers needed a way to speed up the compilation and printing of abstracts and indexes, and they began to use the computer to compile and typeset those materials. When indexes and abstracts that had traditionally been printed were put on a computerized tape to be printed, the same tape could be used for computer searches. One of the first organizations to use this technique was the National Library of Medicine, which computerized the production of *Index Medicus* in the mid-1960s and began the MEDLARS (Medical Literature Analysis and Retrieval System) files (Henry et al. 1980, p. 2).

Currently, government agencies, professional societies, and commercial publishers are the major producers of databases. Although some producers permit direct access to their product, most sell the databases to commercial vendors, who serve as middlemen between the producers and the users. The vendors most commonly dealt with in academic libraries are Lockheed (DIALOG), SDC (ORBIT), and BRS (Lamb 1981, p. 80). Each vendor offers a different selection of databases (although many of the most widely used are offered by more than one vendor), and each uses a distinct command language to instruct the computer to perform the search. The spread of online database searching was hastened with the development of telecommunications networks like Tymnet and Telenet, which reduced the costs of telecommunications involved in online database searches.

In 1982, the entire connect-time use for online services totaled 1.3 million hours, and $127 million was spent on the services. In that year, legal institutions used the online services most, followed by industry, then government. Academic libraries were fourth (Williams 1984, p. 1). Although academic libraries were early users of online search services, use in college and university libraries has grown more slowly than in commercial and governmental libraries, perhaps because:

Faculty members are conservative and cautious in their approach to new information-gathering methods, preferring to rely on time-proven methods such as talking with colleagues through the "invisible college" network and sending low-paid graduate students to the library to search the literature manually. After receiving the results of one

"Faculty members are conservative and cautious in their approach to new information-gathering methods."

good online search, however, many faculty become "hooked" on this new method of finding information (Hoover 1980, p. 16).

Cost is undoubtedly another reason that many faculty and students have not used online services. Both the direct and indirect costs associated with online searching can be considerable. The direct costs include the vendor's charge for the connect-time and/or the information units delivered, the telecommunications cost, and the printing cost. The indirect costs include primarily staff time but can also involve training costs, equipment purchase or rental, the cost of searching aids, and general institutional overhead. Most libraries do not charge for the staff time involved but do charge the user the direct charges of searching. The way the cost of online searching is structured varies among academic libraries. In a survey of approximately 50 libraries, almost all the libraries charged some fee for online searching, but in some institutions library funds are used to subsidize the cost (Lamb 1981). The greatest number charged a rate sufficient to recover costs, although in a few cases users (especially off-campus users) paid an amount above the actual cost of the search (Lamb 1981, p. 79).

The appropriateness of charging for online searches is somewhat controversial because most other library services are offered free of charge to users (Smith and Knapp 1981), and libraries in this country have a proud tradition of free access to information. Unfortunately, most library budgets are not large enough to absorb the cost of free online searches and so libraries have had to pass along the direct charges to patrons. In libraries where searches have been free or highly subsidized, the demand for the services has skyrocketed. Although studies have shown that patrons who need information are not opposed to paying for online searches, it is true especially of users in commercial and industrial libraries and of well-funded researchers (Hoover 1980, p. 24). Students and researchers working in areas where grant monies are difficult to obtain are often forced to curtail their use of the services. The problem is not considered acute as long as a print equivalent to the database is available and users have an alternative method of gathering information—albeit a more time-consuming one. Some very valuable databases, such as Smithsonian Scientific Information Exchange, do not have print counterparts, however, and in some libraries, the subscriptions to little-used periodical indexes are being dropped in favor of exclusive online access (Smith and Knapp 1981, p. 208). Librarians will need to watch closely the issue of charging for online searches to ensure that users are not being denied access to needed information because they cannot afford it. It is hoped that with the growing popularity of such services, the costs to users will decrease.

Users who have become accustomed to online searching have found it very difficult to revert to conventional methods of retrieving information. The advantages of online searching are clear. In the first place, it permits a type of searching that could not be done manually.

> *One example...is a search for the use of computers to control lasers in printing.... There were some 78,000 items on computing, 22,000 on lasers, and 13,000 on printing. The computer search showed that there were six references containing all three items* (Henry et al. 1980, p. 101).

The online search system is able to use the Boolean operators "and," "or," and "not," thus allowing a search for items that contain the terms computers *and* lasers *and* printing. Online search systems can also truncate terms so that, for example, using the term "comput," a searcher can retrieve all items containing terms such as computers, computing, or computation. The flexibility of online searching permits many access points to the data, and the interactive nature of online searching gives the searcher immediate feedback on the relevance of a search so that the search strategy can be modified at any point to make it more effective.

Another advantage of online searching is its speed, even in a situation where only a single topic is being searched. A searcher can get results in a few minutes that would take days to compile manually. Online searches offer access to many more sources of information than are available in the largest libraries. (Users sometimes forget, though, that this comprehensiveness usually extends back only to the date that the database was first made machine readable. Few databases were online before the mid-1960s or early 1970s, and printed sources must be consulted for any review of the literature before that date.) Finally, the online search usually produces more current information than use of the printed equivalent as databases are updated regularly, some even daily.

Most academic libraries provide online searches as part of the reference services department, although some have established separate departments for online searches. In addition to the traditional online searching databases, many libraries now are also using OCLC or RLIN terminals at reference desks to help in bibliographic verification (Droessler and Rholes 1983; Farmer 1982; Miller 1982). More and more libraries are also providing access to nonbibliographic databases, such as numeric databases, textual-numeric databases, properties databases, and full-text databases (Wanger and Landau 1980, p. 172). Technological developments have increased the storage capacity of computers, making the storage of full texts feasible. Many popular encyclopedias are now available online (Williams 1983, p. 105). Certain vendors also provide the full text of a growing number of newspapers and journals.

Because of the expense of online searches and because the systems are still difficult for the new and infrequent user, the normal method of providing access to online searching in academic libraries is to use a trained librarian searcher to act as an intermediary in performing the search. These searchers are familiar with the systems and the different databases and hence more efficient and more cost-effective in performing searches. Usually an individual who wishes to have an online search performed makes an appointment with a searcher for a presearch interview and may sit in during the actual search to help shape the strategy by commenting on the relevancy of the citations obtained.

This pattern may change somewhat in the near future as users do more searches than trained intermediaries (Meadow 1979b). This shift will be precipitated by the recent decision of two of the largest vendors, BRS and DIALOG, to make some of their most popular databases available at a greatly reduced charge if they are used during off-hours. Advertising for these services has been aimed at the individual who has a personal computer and modem available at home or at work. The command language on both systems has been greatly simplified, and users need to learn only a few commands. An experimental project with the BRS/After Dark system showed that a majority of users were enthusiastic about running their own searches (Janke 1983, p. 16). This new development suggests that in the future users might perform many simple searches – either on privately owned microcomputers or in the library on publicly available terminals or microcomputers. The need will undoubtedly continue for trained searchers to handle complicated searches or to perform searches for individuals who have neither the time nor the inclination to do their own. But as microcomputers become more common, as the command languages become more user-oriented, and as the cost of searching becomes less, trained searchers will probably not have sufficient time to handle all the requests, and users will assume much of the responsibility for online searching in academic libraries.

Online Public Access Catalogs

The purpose of a library catalog is to organize a library's collection and to permit easy access to the materials it owns. Throughout the years, the physical form of the library catalog has varied. Book catalogs were common before 1900, but since the turn of the century, the card catalog has become the accepted format in most libraries. While conventional card catalogs are likely to predominate in the near future in most academic libraries, other formats are now being seriously considered.

One of the most exciting developments in catalogs is the public access online catalog, which provides speedy online access to all the library's holdings by means of a computer terminal. Online catalogs serving either a single institution or a group of institutions are now an operational reality, and they are being planned in many other institutions. The Library of Congress has had a form of online catalog since the mid-1970s. Ohio State, Northwestern, and the University of California were leaders in the development of online catalogs for academic libraries. Most large academic libraries have advanced or preliminary plans for instituting such a catalog. Despite the interest, this technology is not nearly as common as that of the bibliographic utilities or of online database searching; in 1983 probably fewer than 300 online public access catalogs were operational in North America (Jones 1984, p. 153).

Although online catalogs are in many respects a technology of the future, they are discussed here not only because so many libraries are involved in planning for them but also because the online catalog is likely to affect library users significantly because they require a fundamental change in the way users get access to information about the local collection. The online catalog will make the computer's retrieval capabilities directly available to library users and will permit users to have access to information in a more decentralized manner.

Two forces have been largely responsible for the great interest in the online catalog. The first is the high cost of maintaining a traditional card catalog, and the second is the implementation of AACR2 (a set of new cataloging rules) and the simultaneous closing of the Library of Congress's card catalog (Matthews 1982a, p. 1067). Maintaining a catalog is very labor intensive. Even though the use of computers cut the costs of producing catalog cards, the cards produced by the computer must still be filed manually. In large libraries especially, an immense amount of time is spent in maintenance—putting new catalog cards into the card catalog and withdrawing the cards of books that have been lost or discarded. Entering records into a computer database would be much more efficient. Instead of manually alphabetizing and filing, the tasks could be accomplished mechanically. The personnel costs of maintaining an online catalog should be much lower than the cost of maintaining a traditional catalog.

The other impetus for libraries' interest in online catalogs came from the adoption of the second edition of the Anglo-American Cataloging Rules (AACR2) and the decision of the Library of Congress to close its catalog concurrently with the adoption of AACR2. Librarians have established descriptive cataloging codes to ensure that a cataloging record created by one cataloger will match that created by another. These cataloging codes have been revised through the years. The latest revision, AACR2, was drawn up by representatives of the American Library Association, the British Library, the Canadian Committee on Cataloging, the Library Association (United Kingdom), and the Library of Congress; it was first published in 1978. In the past as the codes changed, libraries usually adopted a policy of integrating the changes in their existing card catalog by working item by item with cataloging copy provided by the Library of Congress as the Library of Congress was also integrating the new rules and headings into its catalog (Malinconico and Fasana 1979, p. 108).

In 1977, the Library of Congress announced that it would implement AACR2 on January 1, 1980, and close its card catalog at the same time. Libraries reacted to the decision with dismay, protesting that they had had insufficient time to plan for the transition. The Library of Congress then delayed the implementation for one year to give libraries more time to decide how to respond to the changes. The Library of Congress's decision significantly affected all libraries because the adoption of AACR2 meant a large number of cards produced under the new code would have different catalog headings from cards produced under the old code. Because it planned to begin using an automated catalog after the implementation of AACR2, the Library of Congress would not need to integrate new headings and cataloging into an existing catalog and would be freer to make the large number of changes necessary to cope with AACR2. Other libraries would have two choices: to attempt to maintain a single integrated file and resolve resulting conflicts between existing and new forms of catalog entries without the help of the Library of Congress, or to close their old catalogs and begin new ones that would contain only items cataloged using AACR2. (The option to continue cataloging using AACR1 was not a serious consideration because the Library of Congress provides so much of the original cataloging in this country and because any library that chose to retain the old cataloging rules would have to rely entirely on its own original cataloging as its bibliographic data would not be compatible with the national databases.)

Debates raged in the literature about whether it would be better to close the old catalogs and begin new ones — either traditional card catalogs or alternatives like COMs or online catalogs — or to try to integrate AACR2 records into the existing catalogs (Association of Research Libraries 1978; Hewitt and Gleim 1979). Academic libraries made different decisions about what to do, but regardless of their choices, the implementation of AACR2 coupled with the closing of the Library of Congress's catalog served as a catalyst for many libraries to explore seriously the possibility of an alternative form of library catalog.

Many libraries that did close their catalogs created COM catalogs, which presented problems for the users because they usually required looking both in the annual updated catalog and in a supplement. Many users looked in only one, assuming that if an item did not appear, the library did not have the item (Beckman 1982, p. 2044). And, as with most types of microforms, users who found the readers difficult to operate or who had trouble reading the type resisted using them. Most libraries with COM catalogs view COM as an interim step on the way to a public access online catalog (Matthews 1982a, p. 1067).

The online catalog has great appeal for both librarians and users. It substantially reduces the costs of maintaining a card catalog. It can, if integrated with other technical service files, streamline and permit reorganization of the work done in technical services departments. Many current paper files could be eliminated, and, because support work for technical services could be performed from any terminal, decentralization would be possible (Freedman 1984, p. 1202). Having the catalog online would also reduce the space required in the library to house the catalog, although much of that space would be needed to use public access terminals.

This type of catalog offers equal promise for the users. Although no one agrees yet about what features should be included in an online catalog, it should provide at minimum the same access points provided by the card catalog. The online catalog has the potential for increasing the number of points of access to the library's holdings; it can go beyond title, author, and subject by using entry points such as the international standard book number or key words in the title. The computer also offers powerful searching techniques for combining and restricting searches. For instance, a user could look at entries in just one language or in just one time period. Some catalogs permit multiple word/concept searching using the Boolean operators "and," "not," and "or." In some systems, the online catalog not only identifies holdings but also has the ability to indicate the location and the status of items checked out (for instance, "reported lost," "on reserve," "at the bindery"). Last, the entire catalog can be distributed to a number of locations, within the library itself and outside the library. Dial-in access is possible so that individuals with personal computers in their homes or offices could have access without coming to the library (Matthews 1982b, p. 4).

With other features added, the online catalog could provide still more services, especially if the online catalog were part of an integrated system and if it permitted access to the resources of more than one library.

Potentially an online catalog is considerably more than the traditional card catalog executed in a different medium. The terminals used for an online catalog can provide entree to a broad array of information services. They can provide information about the holdings of an entire consortium of cooperating libraries in addition to information about local holdings. The same terminals, with appropriate restrictions, can also be used to borrow a copy of a desired item or to secure a reproduction of a brief document from a distant source. The use of such a terminal need not be restricted to the information contained in the catalog. The same terminal could also be used to access a variety of remote, online database services. Communication with a serial record system is a possibility, and that could allow users to deter-mine quickly whether a citation found in an online database can be consulted locally. The terminal could, of course, communicate with a circulation system to determine whether an item is available, or with an acquisition system to deter-mine if it is on order (Malinconico 1984, p. 1213).

Although the number of public access online catalogs in operation is still limited, studies are being done to assess crit-ical issues and problems in designing, developing, and oper-ating public access online catalogs and to determine what features would be the most useful for library patrons (Ferguson et al. 1982; Moore 1981). One of the most encouraging results of these studies is that users like online catalogs. A nationwide Online Patron Access Project spon-sored by the Council on Library Resources found that more than 90 percent of users surveyed had a favorable attitude toward the online catalog. Ninety percent also stated that the online catalog was better than the manual catalog (Fayen 1983, p. 84). More research needs to be done to define users' needs in terms of what the new technology will allow so that the online catalog will be a clear improvement upon the card catalog it replaces. Research also needs to address such fundamental cataloging issues as a subject access and authority control in online systems. "The current interest in research on computer catalogs is fortunate at this stage of their develop-ment when so few libraries have them. Not only can other librarians, if they are smart, take advantage of the experiences of the pioneers, but a good deal of standardization can be post-poned until more knowledge is gained" (Broadus 1983, p. 458).

Although online catalogs have some clearcut advantages, their implementation involves some obvious problems. The most obvious is the initial capital investment and the ongoing costs of maintaining the computer. Another disadvantage is that the use of the catalog then becomes dependent upon the computer system's remaining operational. Unless a library provides some sort of backup catalog (or backup computer), the library would be without the use of the catalog when the computer malfunctions (Matthews 1982b, p. 13).

Another cost involved in online catalogs is the cost associated with the retrospective conversion of all the catalog records that are not currently in machine-readable form. Any library that inaugurates an online catalog without retrospective conversion will face the problem of forcing users to consult two catalogs to gain access to the library's complete holdings. Librarians will need to decide whether retrospective conversion is feasible based on the size of the collection, the percentage of records in machine-readable form, and the users' needs for older material. Although many options are currently available for handling retrospective conversion, it is undeniably expensive. The University of Pennsylvania, for example, estimates it will cost $1.8 million to make all its catalog records machine readable (De Gennaro, 1984a, p. 4).

By the end of this century, it is very probable that online catalogs will be standard in all but the smallest academic libraries. The catalog will most likely be just one component of an integrated system that will support all library operations. The rapid advances in minicomputers and microcomputers accompanied by significant decreases in the costs of those systems will make integrated systems possible in most libraries. Libraries then will truly be "reinvented," and the "electronic library" will be common in colleges and universities.

The Electronic Library

The term "electronic library" has come into vogue to describe the library of the future (Cline and Sinnott 1983; Dowlin 1984). Libraries have traditionally been viewed as repositories of knowledge, generally in the form of books or other printed material. As the need for access to information grows and as the means of transmitting information changes, libraries must put aside their traditional role to survive in an electronic age. To remain relevant to society, libraries must change and, if they cannot make the transition, they will soon be relegated to the function of archival storage—a place to go to seek knowledge of the past. The new technologies have opened up a new world for libraries, and many are already exploring this new world.

The transition is made harder because libraries cannot wholly abandon their traditional mission as a keeper of books. At least to the end of this century, it seems clear that print materials will continue to coexist with electronic information. Research libraries will likely always need to maintain a large collection of books for archival purposes.

The transition period to the new electronic library will not be easy for either librarian or user. Many librarians may have trouble adapting to a working environment very different from that in which they began their careers, and some may resist technological change (Fine 1980). Without extensive retraining, some librarians may suffer occupational displacement as the modus operandi of librarianship changes (Veaner 1984, p. 625). Many users will also have trouble adapting to the changes. "This era of technical innovation in libraries has become for patrons an age of discontinuity of library services as library practices they have grown accustomed to are rapidly replaced by new ones" (Jones 1984, p. 151). Despite the advantages of online catalogs, for example, some patrons still prefer a drawer of three-by-five cards because they are familiar with that type of catalog.

No clearcut picture yet indicates what the academic library of the electronic age will be. More than one variety will doubtless exist because the institutions of higher education these libraries serve are so diverse. Some indications of the future can be discerned from academic libraries that have already begun to explore nontraditional means of providing library services, however.

Brown University is one of the so-called "Star Wars" universities, those institutions of higher education that are pioneering in information technology for instructional purposes. Brown has launched a 10-year program to design and install 10,000 "scholars' workstations" at a projected cost of $50 million to $70 million. At the completion of this project, Brown will be a "wired university" with enough workstations available to serve all faculty and students. "In the beginning, the workstations will provide secretarial functions, but soon, as libraries and other databases become accessible to computers, the workstations could be used more like research assistants" (Tucker 1983–84, p. 12). When the workstations are fully operational, many services that are now available only in libraries will be available to users of the workstations, including access to the library's catalog and other bibliographic and nonbibliographic databases.

The role of the library will change in this type of environment. Its services will be available in a much more decentralized fashion, and users will not have to come to a physical entity, "the library," to use its resources. The use of the library as a study hall or reading room will possibly decline. The library would still play a vital role in selecting and disseminating information and would continue to serve as an intermediary between a user in need of specific information and the sources of that information. Librarians might also assist in the design of local information systems and participate in the planning of information networks.

The director of libraries at Brown, Merrily Taylor, has noted, "If the university has a basic commodity that it both trades in and lives off, it's information. You can't conceive of a place like Brown without its library. If the library was gone, would you still have a university? We're a fundamental resource" (Tucker 1983–84, p. 13). Taylor also points out, however, the troubling issue that as increased computerization is incorporated in the library, the library resources may no longer be free to users. At this point, the use of bibliographic databases is available free of charge at Brown, but as more reference materials are put online, the policy will have to be reexamined. She raises the question about what it means when the information society produces haves and have-nots, depending on who can pay for the information needed but expresses the hope that Brown and other universities might be able to cooperate and acquire databases of their own and mount them on university computers so that information would be available to people in the university community without charge (Tucker 1983–84, p. 13).

Another example of a library that has been reshaped by computerization is Clarkson College's Educational Resources Center (ERC). When the center was opened in 1980, it was billed as "the most modern computer library in the country." According to Robert Plane, Clarkson's president:

> Clarkson entered the future with the opening of the ERC ...because of its willingness to face the Information Revolution, to search for answers through a multidimensional array of computer information.... I love museums, but we're not in the eighties unless we get over the idea that a library resembles a museum (Horner 1981, p. 657).

The library was designed to make as close a union as possible between the computer and the library's library function; the hub of the ERC is an IBM 4341 computer. Although the ERC still contains many books, librarians and users rely greatly on the retrieval of computer information. The ERC also emphasizes microforms of all types and audiovisual materials (Horner 1981). Clarkson is a good example of what automation is possible in the libraries of smaller institutions.

Many other academic libraries are making progress into the electronic age. Cline and Sinnott (1983) have written in-depth case studies of four others, exploring the impact of these new technologies on libraries and their users. The rapid developments in microcomputer software and hardware and the increased demand for computer use are affecting almost all academic libraries (Guskin, Stoffle, and Baruth 1984). Libraries are taking many different paths to the information age, and, as in any enterprise, the pioneers will make some costly mistakes. No easy answers explain how best to make the changes necessary to ensure that libraries remain viable into the twenty-first century, but the efforts of the pioneers will make it easier for those who come after them to make the transition.

To date, the number of libraries that are in the process of building an "information age" library is still small. Most have not yet taken the initial steps, and many have not yet even begun the hard task of planning for change. But long-range planning, especially planning to meet the costs of technological change, is essential if technology is to be successfully integrated into the library. Libraries and their supporting institutions must make plans for an expensive transformation at a time when funds are already limited and when many other demands are competing for them. It is hard to measure the projected costs against established patterns, because many of the expenditures are needed for costly but nonoptional supplements to present services rather than as substitutes. "In short, a comprehensive and imaginative effort seems required to provide the economic backdrop for the technology revolution if universities are to guide a successful library transformation in a fiscally responsible way" (Council on Library Resources 1983, pp. 20–21).

Technology has a strong appeal, but it cannot be adopted willy-nilly only for the sake of change. Much thought has to go into decisions about how technological change can best be implemented and how the promise of technology can best be fulfilled. "Libraries should not make technology the issue. Technologies are tools to be employed for the benefit of users and in the attainment of the service and process objectives of the library" (Jones 1984, p. 154). Technologies that do not contribute to these aims are superfluous.

Librarians must ask themselves some very hard questions and must reexamine their basic assumptions if they want to stay in business (Matheson 1984). "Librarians are automating, but the key question is what are we automating for. Unfortunately, most of the time, it is to do the same thing better and faster rather than do new things" (p. 208). Automation is not enough. Librarians may need to abandon certain assumptions and mindsets, remaining flexible about the purpose of libraries in this new environment.

Libraries must adapt to survive but there are reasons to be optimistic:

For centuries, [libraries] have been bound by what mankind could do to collect, classify, and disseminate information using laborious, time-consuming methods. Now, at last, libraries can escape those limitations if they have the courage and the foresight to do so. For the first time ever, lack of proper technology is no longer an obstacle. The computer power, data base storage, and software are all available to provide the desired services. What remains for libraries to do is to see that they are on the threshold of a new world; to be open to new ideas about how information may be produced, distributed, retrieved, and used; to let users tell them what they need and then to provide those services as quickly, capably, and cheaply as possible (Fayen 1983, p. 111).

It is a tall order, but with planning, research, imagination, and the commitment of sufficient resources, it can be achieved.

THE MANAGEMENT OF ACADEMIC LIBRARIES

The single most important challenge facing the academic library manager is securing constructive change and improvement in library performance. Any organization must grow and develop in order to successfully accommodate a changing environment, and libraries are no exception. If libraries are to succeed as active partners in the instructional and research programs of universities, they must be sensitive to changing conditions both within their internal structure and in the external environment. . . . Furthermore, the library must move toward a more assertive role within the community it serves, influencing university plans, programs, and priorities rather than simply coping with events as they occur (Webster 1977, p. 83).

The management of academic libraries has become increasingly important over the last 20 years, partly because of their growing size and complexity. It has also, however, been an outgrowth of the financial dilemma faced by academic libraries as the demand for their services has increased, the cost of library materials has exceeded the rate of inflation, and library budgets have stabilized or declined.

The fortunes of academic libraries always mirror the fortunes of their parent institutions. During the 1960s, libraries experienced a golden decade of funding. Administrators were sought for their ability to handle growth and expansion — of budgets, of collections, of staffs. Today, the manager of an academic library faces a different agenda, and the problems he or she must confront are associated with managing an institution during a period of austerity. Administrators must confront the challenge to maintain operations, services, and collections in the face of rising costs and relatively stable or declining budgets. Planning, especially making choices and setting priorities for the expenditure of increasingly limited resources, has become of utmost importance.

The long-term promise of automation requires library directors to find funds for automation in already tight and essentially fixed budgets. To cover the cost of automation, hard choices may have to be made to cut existing programs or services. It is much more difficult to introduce change into an organization when to do something new requires deemphasizing or discontinuing something old and reallocating the existing resources. Inevitably the something old will be someone's vested interest because "everything that libraries do is important to someone: to the library staff because it can

Planning, especially making choices and setting priorities for the expenditure of increasingly limited resources, has become of utmost importance.

mean their jobs; to faculty because they want their specific areas of research well supported by the collection; to students because they need library materials and services to achieve good grades" (Webster 1977, p. 78). Knowing which of the library's services have become obsolete is equally important to knowing the needs of the library's users (Drucker 1976). The manager must ask an unpopular question: "What can be abandoned in order to reallocate resources to something that isn't getting done?" (p. 7).

Library directors, now more than ever before, have to demonstrate the importance of the library to the educational mission of the parent institution. No other element of the university serves so many diverse constituencies, and the university as a whole has to be convinced of the importance of the library to its users. Increasingly, the library director is called on to serve as an advocate for the library, and the most effective library directors are those with the political acumen to gain support for the library not just within the college or university but in the larger world. "One of the greatest benefits a library administrator can provide for a staff is to perform so well politically that the library staff will have an adequate share of the institution's resources to meet their responsibilities" (Govan 1977, pp. 264–65).

The change in the managerial requirements of academic libraries has resulted in a need for a new type of administrator. Library directors in the past were often selected because they were scholars and bibliophiles. Occasionally chosen from the teaching faculty, the director of a few decades ago sometimes had a doctorate but no degree in library science. Traditionally, the directorship, like the presidency of an academic institution, was a lifelong post in which the incumbent remained until retirement. The 1960s marked the beginning of change in this pattern, and since then, libraries have not been directed by the same type of people nor has the tenure of the director been so secure. The role of the university library director has changed markedly, and the position of director has become increasingly difficult to hold (McAnally and Downs 1973). In the large academic libraries belonging to the Association of Research Libraries (ARL), "one-half of the directors were found to have changed within the past three years, four of them twice" (p. 103). Both external and internal pressures contribute to the problem—among them pressures from the president's office, from the library staff, from faculty, and from students. In conjunction with a declining ability to meet users' needs, a lack of cohesive library planning, and an institutional inability to accommodate change, these difficulties had contributed to the increasing burdens on the library director.

Library directors now are chosen primarily for their demonstrated managerial competence and leadership. A recent study compared ARL directors in 1981 to the directors of the same libraries in 1966 and found some interesting differences between the two groups. In 1966, 15 percent of the directors lacked library degrees, but by 1982, every ARL director had earned a graduate library degree. The number of female directors had increased. In 1966, only one ARL library was headed by a woman; by 1981, 12 (14 percent) had female directors. The proportion of directors with doctorates fell from nearly half in 1966 to one-third in 1981. The directors of these prestigious libraries were still predominantly middle-aged males, but the evidence suggests that competition for directorships had intensified because of an enlarged pool of potential candidates. "The genteel, scholarly, even dilettantish directors of the past are yielding to career-minded managers, administrators, and technicians" (Karr 1984, p. 285).

The modern library director faces many critical issues (many of which are discussed in the following section on personnel). Among the other issues that the director must confront are those relating to organization of the library and budgeting.

The Organization of Academic Libraries
The appropriate organization of academic libraries is now considered to be one of the most important aspects of library management—but such was not always the case. The history of academic libraries contains little information about library organization before the late 1930s and early 1940s (Dunlap 1976, p. 395). Administration in even the largest academic libraries was highly centralized until that time, and the organization was structured as it had been when the institution was much smaller. As libraries grew, this highly centralized organization became cumbersome and hard to administer. The exact point where organization becomes a problem in libraries is not known, but it has been suggested that when a library's collection reaches 200,000 volumes, organizational problems begin to emerge and should be recognized as a separate element in administration (McAnally 1952).

Academic libraries today are organized in many different patterns, depending upon size, kind of institution, growth rate, geographic dispersal, and available space. Regardless of the organizational pattern chosen, almost all academic libraries are structured in a hierarchical manner. Although some small college libraries have experienced success using a collegial organization (Bechtel 1981), the large number of professional and nonprofessional employees in most libraries has led nearly all of them to adopt an administrative structure consisting of a director and a number of middle managers.

As recently as the 1940s, almost all college and university libraries, regardless of size, were organized along departmental lines. Work was apportioned among various departments — circulation, reference, and cataloging, for example — and all department heads reported to the chief librarian. As libraries grew in size, the number of departments grew also, until the span of control was so wide that either administration began to break down or else the chief librarian became so involved in operational duties that no time was left for broader responsibilities such as planning or institutional relationships. Large libraries tried various ways of reorganizing, but by the early 1950s, one particular plan of organization had been widely accepted in large libraries: the bifurcated organization based on a division of library functions into readers' services and technical services (McAnally 1952, pp. 21–22). An assistant or associate library director was placed in charge of each of these areas and made responsible to the director for its operation. This bifurcated organization, with some local variations, is still the most commonly used administrative organization in large libraries, while most smaller libraries continue to be organized departmentally.

Academic libraries have always had the problem of the proper balance to be struck between the efficiencies of library service provided in a centralized location and the desire to provide better and more personalized access to a constantly growing library through decentralized units. One of the earliest attempts to provide specialized services to readers was found in the development of departmental or branch libraries, which were often established as the central library became more crowded and as the geographical spread of the campus became larger. By the beginning of the twentieth century, many universities had opened departmental libraries that were separate from the central library and were sometimes administered and maintained by the academic departments they served (Dunlap 1976, p. 398). Today many universities, notably Harvard, still have a large number of departmental libraries, but in many institutions the trend has been away from departmental collections, especially at those libraries that have been hard hit by budget cuts. Departmental libraries remain the "most persistent and difficult organizational problem for the director of a university library" (Rogers and Weber 1971, p. 73) and continue to challenge library administrators as they have for years. Under the present circumstances of proliferating academic departments and increasing interdisciplinary research, "the unbridled creation of branch libraries would be a disservice to users unless financial resources were to permit complete duplication of materials and service hours (but the resources never do)" (pp. 73–74). Pressures for departmental libraries remain strong on campuses because users generally prefer the greater convenience and accessibility they provide to a centralized library, however efficient it may be.

In many large libraries, another decentralized pattern of organization can be seen in the establishment of a separate library for undergraduate students. Although Harvard's Lamont Library was built in 1949, the real burst of interest in such libraries came in the 1960s and early 1970s. The undergraduate libraries were designed to provide services to undergraduates in large academic institutions on a level appropriate to their academic needs and in a separate facility so they would not have to compete with graduate students and faculty. The interest in establishing new undergraduate libraries has diminished, however. Many librarians believe the need for undergraduate libraries has been alleviated because most central libraries now provide intensive instructional programs for all library users (Person 1982). The future place of undergraduate libraries is not clear. It is probable that undergraduate libraries will be maintained by the largest and most prosperous university libraries, but the problem of declining resources may make it hard for many library administrators to justify the existence of a separate library for undergraduates, especially if enrollments decline significantly.

Academic libraries continue to experiment with different organizational patterns in attempts to balance the desire to bring the best service possible to users with the reality of a finite amount of funds to be spent on those services. To date, the perfect organizational structure has yet to be developed, and surely no *one* perfect organizational structure would suit all libraries. The new technologies will doubtless have a major effect on the organizational patterns of libraries, but at this point one can merely speculate about what their impact will be. Some of the arguments in favor of centralization will almost certainly disappear with the advent of new methods of document storage and retrieval and the growth of various online systems. Atkinson (1984) predicts that the organizational pattern of the academic library of the future is likely to be a decentralized one (p. 113), noting that patrons have always preferred specialized or small local library units, and he agrees that the "ideal library is one with one or two librarians, one or two library clerks, a handful of student assistants, a homogeneous identifiable clientele, and a collection large enough to suit that clientele" (p. 113). The academic library of tomorrow, according to Atkinson, will be comprised of a number of these smaller units. The emergence of an increasing number of smaller decentralized units will require a different administrative structure, with the central administrator serving as a coordinator rather than a supervisor, and will require an extraordinarily talented administrative staff to avoid conflict.

> There will no doubt be a long period of negotiation and experimentation with a good number of failures and retreats as the library community slowly sorts out what is to become traditional library activity.... One can already see the beginnings of new pressures and new organizational patterns with the advent of high density optical digital discs, carbon fiber optics, and satellite communications, which provide even more distance independence and the potential for storage of large volumes of material in many remote locations so inexpensively that the very existence of a central store of data can be open to doubt. The rise of good, inexpensive, rapid long-distance electronic document transmission may not only change the organizational patterns of individual libraries but may well change the patterns of librarianship as well. What is certain is that library organization will change, and that it will be different from what we expect (Atkinson 1984, p. 114).

In a similar vein, Martell (1983) proposes another plan for restructuring the library—a library organized into small client-centered work groups with librarians operating "at all points where the library interacts with its user groups" (p. 67). Each member of the work group would perform a number of library functions—advanced reference, development of the collection, instruction, original cataloging, and other forms of information service. According to Martell, such a library would be more responsive to users' needs.

Cline and Sinnott (1983), in their study of the effects of automation on the organization of university libraries, speculate that libraries will adopt some form of matrix management (pp. 174–75). They further suggest that libraries may be reorganized with staff grouped according to the fields they serve—natural history, social sciences, and humanities, for example, each of which could be further divided by discipline. In this structure, librarians would also devote a substantial part of their time to delivering reference services to scholars using the part of the collection for which they have responsibility. In such a system, libraries would have to make special provisions for users who need materials that cross disciplines.

If these writers are correct in their assessment of the future organizational structure of academic libraries, libraries may at last be able to provide their users with the decentralized, individualized services they have always preferred.

Budgeting
The fiscal management of libraries has always been difficult because of the imbalance between the costs of services that librarians would like to provide and the resources they have available to meet those costs. Even during the 1960s, libraries never overcame their traditional poverty because the demands made on them by users and the commitments they accepted always exceeded their resources. The chronic imbalance between the library's commitments and resources now, however, "threatens to become a vast gulf with the soaring inflation and declining budgetary support that will likely characterize the 1980s" (De Gennaro 1981, p. 9).

Some university administrators view libraries as "bottomless pits" (Munn 1968, p. 52). From the point of view of the central administration, the budgetary needs of academic libraries are complex, frustrating, and often baffling.

The library consumes resources at a prodigious rate, yet despite the best efforts of presidents and fiscal officers to satisfy its seemingly insatiable appetite for dollars, the results satisfy no one—neither faculty nor students nor the librarians themselves. No matter how much money might be earmarked for the library, it is not clear that it would ever be enough (Galvin and Lynch 1982, p. 1).

The library's fiscal problems are compounded by its inability to generate revenue. Almost all of the library's budget comes from the parent institution. One study reported that the portion of library budgets provided by university funds ranged from a high of 97 percent of the budgets of southern public universities to a low of 83 percent of the budgets of northern private universities. The remainder of the budgets of the libraries comes from gifts and endowments and from state and federal grants (Cohen and Leeson 1979, p. 29). Obviously gifts and endowments constitute a much larger percentage of the budgets of private than of public universities, although public universities are now trying to attract more gifts and endowments. Private foundations sometimes provide grants for specific projects, but foundations cannot be expected to underwrite the normal operating costs of libraries.

The Higher Education Act of 1965 provided federal funds to academic libraries for the purchase of materials (Title II-A), for training and research (Title II-B), and for resource sharing (Title II-C). The funds received from the federal government under this act have dwindled greatly and promise to become still smaller. In fiscal year 1983, for instance, under Title II-A, College Library Resources Program, only $1.9 million was awarded to a total of 2,141 institutions of higher education, with each successful applicant receiving an award of $890. The FY 1984 Appropriations Act does not include funding for the College Library Resources Program, and the Department of Education does not anticipate making awards under the program in 1984 (Fine 1984, p. 243).

The university's budget seems destined to remain the dominant source of support for academic libraries, but because

> . . . a large percentage of university budgets is taken up by relatively fixed costs (tenured faculty, utilities, building maintenance), the likelihood that library budgets can increase substantially through cost savings elsewhere in the university is virtually nil. Thus for the next decade, at least, it seems realistic to assume that universities will not have the resources to increase library budgets substantially; indeed the more likely outcome may be a steady erosion in the real resources available to libraries from their institutions (National Enquiry 1979, p. 146).

The portion of the parent institution's budget that is devoted to the library has remained fairly constant over time. Before

1960, on the average, academic libraries received about 3.1 percent of the parent institution's total budget. During the late 1960s and early 1970s, the figure rose above 4 percent, but after 1976, the percentage drifted down again (Talbot 1984, p. 74). The percentage varies from institution to institution, with large universities typically devoting a somewhat smaller percentage of their budgets to libraries than small colleges do. But in looking at funding patterns over the past 30 years, one is struck by the stability of the percentage of funds devoted to libraries.

The true significance of this invariant pattern lies in what it reveals about academic institutions' budgeting for libraries (Talbot 1984). Apparently library financing is not based upon institutional needs because, if it were, the percentage of the university's budget devoted to the library would be expected to fluctuate widely from year to year. Academic institutions themselves are called upon to respond to many different kinds and types of needs that rarely can be objectively defined and defended. "If this is true for the parent, it must also be true for the library, which is not only a creature of the parent but explicitly charged with supporting some of the academic needs that can neither be 'objectively defined' or 'defended'" (p. 76). Like other academic costs, academic library costs have been determined not by need but by available revenue, which leads to an environment in which there are no absolute standards to be met, only relative or comparative ones. Most academic libraries judge how well they are doing by comparing the size of their collection, staff, and budget to those of libraries in similar institutions. This system of comparison, however, cannot provide a rationale for articulating library needs and matching them to the resources required to meet them (Talbot 1982, p. 37).

Within the library's budget itself, the pattern of expenditure has also remained fairly stable over the past few decades. The typical academic library allocates about 60 percent of its budget for salaries, 30 percent for materials, and 10 percent for other expenses.

A major shift has occurred, however, in expenditures between books and serials within the portion of the budget devoted to materials. In 1970, 62 percent of the acquisitions budget was spent on books and 34 percent on serials; by 1976, the proportion had changed so that only 44 percent of the budget was spent on books and 50 percent on serials (Cohen and Leeson 1979, p. 41). Among members of ARL, expenditures for serials reached a high of 58 percent of total materials expenditures in 1981, falling to 56 percent in 1983 (Association of Research Libraries 1984, p. 7). The drop in expenditures for books in favor of serials can be explained in several ways. Books are considered more expendable than journals because journals are thought to contain more up-to-date information, because librarians are reluctant to discontinue subscriptions to journals that have been held a long time, and because librarians hope that sometime in the future, when budgetary pressures ease, they will be able to replenish their book collections by buying books not purchased when they were first published (Cohen and Leeson 1979, p. 41). Even shifting funds from books to serials has not been sufficient to allow libraries to maintain past levels of acquisition, however. The continuing inflation in the cost of books and journals combined with the rapid and continuing growth of publication mean that most libraries are falling behind in acquisitions, especially purchases of monographs.

In a time of stable or declining budgets, library directors face a hard choice in transferring any other funds to increase the acquisitions budget. The "other" portion of library budgets constitutes 10 percent of the whole, but there is little chance of cutting back there because that portion of the budget is used to finance automation. In many libraries, the "other" budget is in fact increasing, and it may have to go up to 15 or 20 percent to fund technological advances.

The portion of the budget devoted to personnel accounts for about 60 percent of the total budget and is perhaps most tempting to those who seek more funds for acquisition. Although this portion of the budget has remained stable, the number of staff in academic libraries has nonetheless dropped relative to the number of students. Between 1967 and 1978, the number of library staff per 1,000 full-time equivalent students fell from 7.2 to 6.7, with professional staff decreasing from 3.2 to 2.7 and student assistants decreasing from 2.9 to 2.4 per 1,000 FTE students (Talbot 1984, p. 79). A portion of the funds needed to introduce automation has likely already been taken from this portion of the budget.

Many librarians had expected that the introduction of automation would increase productivity and thus reduce personnel costs in libraries. To date, most computer systems have improved services more than they have cut costs, and it is questionable whether automation will ever be able to reduce costs in libraries because of the labor-intensive nature of library operations (Baumol and Blackman 1983). Libraries, like other service industries, are especially vulnerable to a debilitating condition termed "cost disease" (Baumol and Blackman 1983). A library is a labor-inflexible industry because its success requires personal services and depends heavily on human thought and attention. In labor-intensive industries, gains in productivity fail to offset increases in salaries. The hope that as the price of computer hardware fell, the cost of libraries' computerized operations would become increasingly inexpensive relative to conventional procedures has failed to materialize. The evidence to date shows that such a differential has not yet been realized because the decline in prices for computer hardware has increased the proportion of software and other labor-intensive components in the total spent for computer operations. Because of the substantial residue of labor-intensive activities, the electronic library like the conventional library will be vulnerable to "cost disease."

Some libraries, especially those in small liberal arts colleges, may not have the chance to see what automation might be able to do for their operating costs because they are not likely to have the money to invest in full-scale library automation. The libraries at such institutions will shoulder a disproportionate share of the budget cuts because expenditures for library materials are easier to cut than people (Sullivan 1982). The relative unavailability of capital funds means that many institutions will not be able to adopt labor-saving library technology. The best chance for smaller libraries to automate will come through the use of affordable microcomputers.

It is hard to determine where library budgets can be trimmed. In almost every library, the fat has already been cut from the budget. While it is unlikely that the library's share of the parent institution's budget will increase, it is likely that the cost pressures on libraries will increase further.

It will be the task of the library director to convince the institutional administration of the library's central place in everything else the college or university does.

Academic libraries must truly become active participants in the scholarly information transfer process. To discharge that role, however, librarians need the support and understanding of their institutional communities. To obtain that support they must make greater efforts to explain how libraries are being affected by current trends and how libraries should be changed to accommodate them. Changes in the library to

make realistic accommodations to new demands will be
possible only to the extent that the library itself plays a
central role in its parent's response. If libraries remain on
the periphery of institutional response to the information
age, they will become increasingly irrelevant. The success of
librarians in explaining and asserting their present and
potential future role in the scholarly communication process
will determine the degree to which they will receive the
funding they need to adapt realistically to change (Talbot
1984, pp. 80–81).

In sum, directors of academic libraries have historically paid
little attention to environmental factors, concentrating the
greatest part of their energy on internal library matters (Metz
1979, p. 149). Library directors, as the library's key representatives, however, must place a greater emphasis on external relationships within and without the academic community. If the
college or university cannot fund the library sufficiently, the
library may need to raise some of its own support. Although it
alone is unlikely to solve the budget problem, fund raising will
be an increasingly important role of the academic library
director of the future.

Innovative Management in Academic Libraries
"Managing the service institution for performance will increasingly be seen as the central managerial challenge of a
developed society and as its greatest managerial need"
(Drucker 1974, p. 135). To meet the challenge of managing the
library more efficiently and effectively, library managers, like
the managers of most other types of nonprofit organizations,
have tried to use some of the managerial techniques first developed by business and government. Academic libraries have
experimented with managerial techniques such as Management
by Objectives (MBO) and with new budgeting systems such as
Zero-Based Budgeting (ZBB) and Planning Programming
Budgeting System (PPBS). Most of these techniques have been
tried and then discarded. During the early 1970s, for example,
a large number of libraries tried MBO, but not many adopted
it permanently. For libraries, MBO is a limited approach to
management that is not only costly and difficult to implement
but also yields uncertain results (Michalko 1975). In the same
vein, most of the new budgeting systems that libraries tried
were discontinued a short time after implementation, and most
libraries went back to the tried-and-true line-item budget.

Many librarians felt these new techniques did not justify the immense amount of staff time they consumed. Perhaps the new management systems do not work well in libraries because they do not take into account the political environment in which a library operates and the fact that nearly all the important decisions made in a library have an overriding political component (De Gennaro 1978). In a like manner, the more critical the decision, the less useful a cost-benefit analysis is to library decision makers; *political* analysis is important in academic libraries (Raffel 1974).

Although many of these new managerial techniques have not been found appropriate for libraries, planning has become widely accepted, and academic libraries have begun to emphasize it within the last decade. Many large libraries have planning offices, and, in smaller ones, the library director or the administrative group in the library devotes time to this exercise. If libraries hope to make the transition into the information age smoothly, librarians will need to do even more planning. Some libraries have adopted strategic planning techniques and have begun to examine what they do best and who their competition is. Increasingly, the computer center is seen as "a worthy, if not awesome competitor. Disciplines that give higher priority to computing and other resources than to traditional library materials may pose for the library and library dependent faculties a new and increasingly ominous challenge" (O'Neil 1982, p. 8).

As academic libraries have grown in size and complexity, library administration has ceased to be a one-person job. In addition to the line managers found in libraries, most large libraries now include a team of individuals to lend specialized expertise to managerial problems. These specialized administrative positions are filled with individuals knowledgeable about topics such as personnel, budgeting, planning, and automation who are able to assist the director in the management of their specific areas (Association of Research Libraries 1982).

In addition to a larger administrative component, in many institutions the skills of the library staff are used to aid in administration. Most librarians have shown an increasing desire to take part in decisions that affect their jobs and that they are expected to implement. Most academic libraries use committees of various kinds to gather information and recommend actions to the director. Many library directors have also involved the staff directly in managerial studies of various types, especially studies of organizational review and planning. Some libraries have designed their own self-studies, naming committees to deal with specific areas of interest. Many libraries have also undergone self-study programs with the assistance of the Office of Management Studies (OMS) of the Association of Research Libraries. Since 1971, OMS has designed a series of self-study procedures aimed at analyzing and strengthening library programs in management, collections, preservation, and services. Beginning with the Management Review and Analysis Program, a structured self-study designed to help large research libraries identify, describe, and propose needed changes in current organizational practices, OMS has designed a number of other self-study programs for both large and small academic libraries. In 1983, 31 libraries participated in various OMS self-study programs (Association of Research Libraries 1983, p. 4). OMS has also been active in providing training for the library staff's development and for library consultants.

Library directors are more sophisticated and knowledgeable about management now than they have ever been. But they will need to use all the skills they possess and acquire still more to remain successful. At least for the foreseeable future, management issues will continue to challenge the skill and ingenuity of academic librarians. Administrators of academic libraries will need to bring to their positions a commitment to their institution, a willingness to experiment, and the courage to risk failure. Although managing with limited resources will be the task before administrators for the rest of this century, library directors need to seek a positive posture and strive to play a larger role in academic decisions about the future of the academic library. Academic library directors must provide innovative and resourceful approaches to the needs of both the library and its parent institution to ensure that academic libraries maintain a central role in higher education.

PERSONNEL ISSUES IN ACADEMIC LIBRARIES

Nothing will be as important to the quality of library and information services provided to scholars and students within colleges and universities as the quality of people recruited, retrained, retained, and supported to manage and deliver those services in the next two decades (Abell and Coolman 1982, p. 71).

Libraries are labor-intensive organizations (with approximately 60 percent of the total library budget spent on staff costs). In an academic library, the library staff itself consists of three components: the librarians, the support staff, and the student workers. Professional librarians constitute the smallest group of library employees. They typically have earned at least one graduate degree, a master's degree in library or information science, but many academic librarians also hold second master's degrees or doctorates. The professional staff works at predominantly intellectual and nonroutine tasks, those requiring

a special background and education on the basis of which library needs are identified, problems are analyzed, goals are set, and original and creative solutions are formulated for them, integrating theory into practice, and planning, organizing, communicating, and administering successful programs of service to users of the library's materials and services (American Library Association 1970, p. 3).

Libraries are labor-intensive organizations (with approximately 60 percent of the total library budget spent on staff costs).

Professional librarians serve in leadership roles, administering both the total organization and the various departments and subunits, and they assume primary responsibility for providing reference and library instruction programs, developing and managing the collections, and overseeing cataloging.

The support staff's activities cover a wide range of essential work, including the tasks of inputting, coding, and verifying bibliographic data, maintaining book funds, ordering, claiming serials, filing, nonoriginal cataloging, and other tasks that support the library's daily operations. This group of employees consists of workers who have a wide level of skills, ranging from clerical to paraprofessional.

The student assistants are not only usually the most numerous employees in an academic library, but they are also usually the most visible. They perform the routine tasks for which extensive training is not required: checking out books, shelving returned books, and retrieving items from the stacks (Abell and Coolman 1982, p. 73).

In the past few decades, the tasks professional librarians perform have become more clearly demarcated from those done by nonprofessionals, and in many cases tasks that had previously been done by professional librarians have been transferred to members of the support staff. This transfer has been made possible by the increase in the number of staff members in most libraries and by the introduction of technology. In the late nineteenth and early twentieth centuries, the clerical, housekeeping, and intellectual tasks of librarianship were intermingled because library staffs were typically small and librarians performed all types of library activities to maintain services. As libraries and their staffs expanded after World War II, these tasks began to be separated.

In the late seventies and early eighties, clear distinctions were being made between the duties of professional librarians and support staff. The former were able to spend more time fulfilling the information needs of students and faculty, leaving routine operations in many departments to technical assistants and clerks (DePew 1983, pp. 407–8).

Support staff not only took on more of the clerical and housekeeping functions, but as library technology advanced, they were also able to perform other tasks that had previously been undertaken by librarians. The use of bibliographic utilities, for example, has permitted large portions of cataloging formerly done by professionals to be done by support staff.

This movement of task oriented work from the professional staff to the support staff has been under way for at least a generation and has been well documented. The shift illustrates an important social aspect of the "technological imperative" in that once a technology is applied to carry out very complex, routine mental work, that work is driven downward in the work hierarchy, away from professionals, whose work then expands to comprehend new and more challenging responsibilities, such as those librarians now carry out. Thus in losing a "job," the librarians acquired a much more clearly definable professional responsibility. The change has provided magnificent professional enrichment opportunities for librarians and has similarly enriched the jobs of support staff (Veaner 1984, pp. 623–24).

As nonprofessional staff assumed these new responsibilities, their proportion in the total staff expanded. As recently as

1950, the staff of most college and university libraries was composed of 50 to 90 percent professional librarians. In most libraries now, the ratio is usually one professional librarian to two support staff members, and in some large libraries the proportion of professional librarians is still lower (McAnally 1971, p. 42). As library technology advances, it may be feasible to turn over still more functions to support staff, and the ratio of professionals to nonprofessionals may decrease further.

This reassignment of responsibilities has led to some role confusion between professional librarians and support staff and to a growing dissatisfaction on the part of some support staff about their status (Dougherty 1977).

Librarians spend more time away from their "desks." They actively engage in the governance of libraries, and they spend more time at conferences. The tasks they performed must now be performed in their absence by assistants. Although this process of reassignment has created new opportunities for library assistants, the added responsibilities too often have not been accompanied by commensurate rewards (p. 112).

Dissatisfaction over the gap in salaries and other fringe benefits has led many library support staff members to join employee groups or unions. Library administrators must recognize the needs and interests of this large group of workers in academic libraries, particularly paying attention to how their jobs can be made more varied and responsible. A recent interest on the part of some academic librarians in work enrichment programs perhaps will result in greater job satisfaction on the part of library support workers (Martell and Untawale 1983).

If one examines the literature of librarianship for personnel issues that have been most important during the 1970s and 1980s, one would be struck with the amount of writing that has been devoted to an examination of the appropriate role of the academic librarian. More may have been written about the "search for role and status—for the academic librarian's particular mission as differentiated from other academic actors" (Abell 1979, p. 156)—than about any other related topic. Most of this literature is concerned with the appropriate "status" for academic librarians and with the role of individual librarians in the day-to-day governance of the library.

Status of Academic Librarians

The thorny question of the appropriate "status" for academic librarians—should they be classified in the same personnel group as the teaching faculty or should they have some other type of separate status?—has been in the forefront of issues in academic libraries for at least 30 years, and it has yet to be settled satisfactorily. Academic librarians have long sought a larger recognition of their contributions to the work of the colleges and universities they serve. Because the number of librarians working on any one campus is usually very small, librarians sought to ally themselves with the teaching faculty rather than attempt to establish a separate professional identity for themselves, and their "efforts have been chiefly directed toward some form of recognition within the academy, usually the granting of faculty status to librarians" (Sparks 1980, p. 408). The attempt to gain faculty rank and status was supported by the rationale that the work performed by librarians and teaching faculty was similar.

The search for faculty status began over 100 years ago, "when it was felt that the only way librarians could gain respect and legitimacy for their profession was to be judged and accepted by the same standards as teaching faculty" (DePew 1983, p. 407). H. A. Sawtelle (1878) was perhaps the first to express the notion that because academic librarians participated in the teaching process they should be regarded as teachers, noting that a good librarian must inspire and guide students in the use of library materials, a task that requires "no small amount of understanding and skill," and concluding that librarianship "ought not be annexed to a professorship, but be itself a professorship" (p. 162). At that time, several factors impeded efforts to have librarianship viewed as a profession and to grant academic librarians faculty status: the small number of librarians employed in academic libraries, the small size of the collections, the preponderance of "housekeeping" chores, the failure to distinguish between clerical and profes- sional tasks, the predominance of women in library work, the low quality of library education, the attitude of the faculty toward librarians, and the bureaucratic structure of university library administrations (McAnally 1971, pp. 20–22).

Since that time, librarianship has gradually evolved and grown in stature as a profession, hastened by the growth in the size of library collections and staff, the improvement of library education, and the separation of the duties of librarians and support staff. The greater professionalism of librarians can be seen in today's academic libraries. The professional preparation and the quality of the staff have improved markedly. Librarians have assumed the responsibility of providing better service to both faculty and students. Reference service, which once was uncommon, has come to be a standard and heavily used feature in academic libraries (Kaser 1980, p. 47). By the 1960s, the vast increase in publishing had resulted in librarians' taking a much more active role in the selection of library materials. Librarians gradually assumed most of the responsibility for the development of collections, which, up to that point, had been considered a faculty responsibility. Most large libraries appointed collection development officers. A new category of personnel, the subject area specialist, became widespread in large academic libraries. These specialists have advanced training in a subject discipline as well as in librarianship and are able to help select materials, provide specialized reference service, and serve as liaisons to faculty in specific departments (Holley 1976, p. 198). Although interest in bibliographic instruction had been found in academic libraries for almost a century (Tucker 1979, p. 268), during the 1970s library instruction flourished. As libraries and their collections became larger and more complicated, the need grew for students to be taught how to use them. Many librarians devoted an immense amount of time to teaching the use of the library and its bibliographic tools to both graduate and undergraduate students. It became common in colleges and universities for undergraduate students to be required to take separate courses in bibliographic instruction or to have units on the topic included in other required courses, such as freshman English.[1] Academic librarians enlarged the scope of their previous duties and sought ways to fulfill the information needs of faculty and students. They have also undertaken the task of publishing. Not only do they sometimes collaborate with faculty members on such productions as annotated bibliographies, but they also publish independently in librarianship and subject area specialties.

In recognition of this growing professionalism, the number of academic librarians who have been given faculty status has increased steadily. The earliest recorded granting of faculty status occurred at Columbia University in 1911 (Schmidt 1979,

[1]Because of limited space, the topic of bibliographic instruction has not been covered in depth. For a recent comprehensive overview of this topic, see Kirk 1984.

p. 411). The movement for faculty status was helped by the action of the American Association of University Professors, which admitted academic librarians as members in 1956. At that time, the AAUP Council ruled that "librarians of professional status are engaged in teaching and research" and permitted those librarians who held faculty rank to join. By 1957, 738 librarians were members (McAnally 1971, p. 28). Interest in faculty status grew during the late 1950s and 1960s. At the American Library Association (ALA) conference in 1969, a motion was approved in the Association of College and Research Libraries (ACRL) division of ALA establishing as one of its major goals the achievement of full faculty status for all academic librarians. In 1972, ACRL, the Association of American Colleges, and the AAUP issued a Joint Statement on Faculty Status of College and University Librarians urging the granting of faculty status to librarians as well as the same rights, privileges, and responsibilities of faculty members.

On the surface at least, it would appear that academic librarians have made great progress in attaining their goal. A recent study showed that almost 79 percent of all academic librarians now have some sort of faculty status (DePew 1983, p. 407).

What have been the results of this new status? Salaries of academic librarians have risen in the last decade (but not as much as other faculty members), and benefits have improved. The greatest gains, however, have not been monetary. Librarians with faculty status have an increased opportunity for participation in library and university governance. Faculty status has helped the advancement of bibliographic instruction. Opportunities for job security and for leaves have increased. And promotions are more apt to be based on personal qualifications and achievements than on the supervision of others (Stone 1982, p. 38).

Despite these advances, the issue of the appropriate status for academic librarians is not yet settled. The literature is still full of debates on the appropriateness of faculty status for librarians. One of the major problems with faculty status for librarians arises from the fact that few of the 79 percent of academic librarians who are classified as faculty actually have full faculty status. "Faculty status" is a term loosely defined, and many librarians who are considered to have faculty status actually have "academic" status, which is usually defined as possessing some but not all of the usual faculty privileges. In most instances, librarians have taken on the responsibilities of faculty status without all the benefits. Academic librarians rarely have salaries comparable to teaching faculty, and only a few have academic year rather than calendar year appointments. In most libraries, librarians still work a fairly structured 35- to 40-hour week, so the majority of the typical librarian's time is involved in providing services to patrons and in library operations. Librarians also have found it more difficult to get sabbatical leaves and research funds.

Increasingly, however, academic librarians have been reviewed for promotion and tenure using the same criteria as the teaching faculty or using a modified version of the criteria for faculty. A recent survey of ARL libraries found that librarians with faculty status were characteristically required to meet two distinct sets of criteria, "one set designed to measure performance as librarians, and the other set designed to measure performance as faculty" (English 1983, p. 204). The requirement for research and publication has put academic librarians working 35 to 40 hours per week, 11 months of the year, at a major disadvantage (Payne and Wagner 1984, p. 138). They have little time for engaging in the research and writing for publication usually associated with faculty status, and some competent and dedicated librarians have consequently been denied tenure because they have not published enough.

Not only are librarians at a disadvantage in regard to the time available for research, but many librarians in addition have had no training in research. As most librarians come into entry-level positions with a master's degree in library science as their only graduate degree, those hired by institutions that will evaluate them by standards used for teaching faculty are placed in a difficult position. In addition to research, publishing, and service, many academic institutions now require that faculty librarians have a second degree to qualify for tenure, and many librarians find it virtually impossible to meet all these standards in the 5½ years they have available before the tenure review. Many question the appropriateness of faculty status for librarians because it creates tensions that obscure the proper role of librarians and interferes with the effective delivery of library services by diverting librarians' energies and attentions (DePew 1983, p. 409). The feeling is fairly widespread that academic librarians have assumed the dual responsibilities of a teaching faculty member and a professional librarian to the detriment of the library profession.

Some other opponents of faculty status have based their criticisms upon sociological arguments, viewing the quest for faculty status as a misdirected plea for recognition. The faculty status of academic librarians has been described as an "organization fiction" that has been adopted for librarians for three reasons: to provide a more comforting self-image, to buttress a status claim, and to interpret the profession to the world outside it (Wilson 1979, p. 152). According to Wilson, purpose, behavior, and education are vastly different for academic librarians and teaching faculty, and as a result faculty do not recognize academic librarians' claim to faculty status. She sees the "organization fiction" harming librarianship because it presents librarians with "an inconsistent self-image. A professional identity that is understandable and believable cannot be developed on such a base" (p. 160).

Faculty status still has its strong proponents, however. It seems to have worked best in those few institutions where the commitment to full faculty status for librarians is strong — where librarians are bound by the rules, regulations, and procedures but also enjoy the concomitant benefits of the teaching faculty. At the University of Illinois, for example, librarians have full faculty status and have found "the principles of collegiality, academic freedom and tenure, and the concept of the librarian as a teacher and researcher to be viable and highly beneficial to the academic library environment" (Sewell 1983, p. 212).

Without a doubt, many colleges and universities have had difficulty in determining the proper roles and responsibilities for the librarian who is also a faculty member. It is also true that many academic librarians are troubled as they "try to cope with the difficulties of wearing the hats of two professions" (DePew 1983, p. 408). What options are available to academic librarians with regard to the resolution of their status in academic libraries? Three choices are possible: (1) muster the discipline necessary to accept the values of the academy and work individually and organizationally to meet them; (2) admit that there is nothing wrong in viewing librarianship as a highly skilled vocation rather than as a profession; or (3) establish a quasi-professional category between civil service and faculty status (Axford 1977, p. 277). A fourth alternative would be to have librarians organize as a separate academic group and to seek recognition and status as librarians (Cieslicki 1982, p. 80; DePew 1983, p. 412; Miller 1981, p. 131). This alternative would have the advantage of affirming the goals and objectives of librarianship as an independent profession. Under this new "librarian" status, librarians would be judged by criteria appropriate to their own profession and not those more appropriate for another. This choice would involve setting strict standards on performance, education, and professional competence if librarians want to compel respect from their faculty colleagues.

The situation today is in a state of flux.

For the present, ... the reality is that the mass of college and other academic librarians will continue the tantalizing quest for faculty status, which they will assume to be their only proper aspiration. Faculty status will be much wished for by librarians, but rarely attained and imperfectly real-ized. Academic status, in its various forms, will continue to be the norm. College librarians will remain becalmed on this motionless sea until some strong wind sweeps through academia, giving them new direction in their quest for status and a sense of professional identity (Miller 1981, pp. 132–33).

Participation in Governance

Academic librarians have moved with a clearer sense of direc-tion in their quest for participation in library governance. In the past, academic libraries were organized in a traditional hierarchical structure, and the normal management style was authoritarian, with the director making all decisions in matters pertaining to the library. Today's directors are finding tradi-tional management styles to be less effective, however, as librarians demand increased input into the decisions being made in the organization. Those demands have forced directors to move toward a more open organization with wider staff involvement in decision making.

Maurice Marchant (1976) was one of the first to write about the benefits of greater participation by librarians in the gover-nance of academic libraries. Using 22 large academic libraries as the source of data, Marchant measured the relationship between the degree of librarians' participation in management and five factors: (1) the staff's job satisfaction, (2) the extent of long-range planning in the library, (3) uniformity in library evaluations, (4) circulation of materials for home use, and (5) faculty evaluation of library services, facilities, and resources. In brief, Marchant concluded that the "empirical data in this study supported the thesis that involvement by the university library staff in the library's administration produces greater staff job satisfaction and, through it, better libraries" (p. 164).

Many other writers have explored the topic — some favoring greater participation and some expressing a contrary view. Those who favor greater participation (Dickinson 1973; Webster and Gardner 1975) usually base their opinions on their beliefs that the rank and file library staff benefit by having a chance to participate in the governance of the library, that better decisions are made with staff involvement, and that librarians' greater satisfaction will lead to better library service. Those writers who take the opposite view (Dickinson 1978; Govan 1977; Kaplan 1973) support their stand by concentrating on the inexperience of most librarians in management, the amount of time that would be consumed by participation, and the inappropriateness of the participative model as a means of running a complex service organization.

One of the factors that has contributed to the controversy may have been the lack of understanding about what employee participation actually involves. "Its advocates seldom defined their term. Participation in what? To what degree? To what purpose?" (Govan 1977, p. 259). The misunderstanding centers largely around the amount of participation desirable; even some of the critics of participative management are not against some measure of staff involvement in library governance.

Participative management or power sharing should not — and cannot, if it is to be successful — mean an abdication of responsibility for the library on the part of administrators and managers in the name of democracy. . . . What seems to be required instead is extensive and intensive consultation between administration and staff, but with the ultimate decision-making authority and attendant accountability unequivocally lodged with the library administration (Dickinson 1978, p. 261).

Few advocates of participative management have ever suggested that libraries could be run by majority rule or that the administration should abdicate responsibility and allow the staff to do whatever they please. Most proponents of the system have seen it as a way to force "decision-making down to the level best suited to it by virtue of the availability of relevant information and the effect of the decision on the operation" (Stone 1982, p. 36). Most librarians desiring input into decision making are aware that the director bears ultimate responsibility in administration because of his or her accountability for the operation of the library.

The current status of participation in the management of libraries is best summarized as requiring synthesis between support and criticism.

> *Perhaps in Hegelian fashion, having swung between support and criticism of participatory management, librarians are finding a synthesis on which they can agree. No one seriously questions that properly implemented and maintained, participatory management generally increases staff morale and job satisfaction. "Proper implementation" usually means active support for the technique by top library administrators and phased adoption. It also implies that librarians understand the limits of their involvement and that such participation will not solve all library problems or guarantee happiness with all decisions. Conflicts will still arise and difficult decisions will still have to be made. . . . Finally librarians will have to accept that participatory management is no substitute for individual responsibility and leadership. There will likely always be library directors and just as likely they will be paid considerably more than the rest of the non-administrative staff. . .because they are accountable for the operation of the library* (Burckel 1984, p. 32).

Although a few authoritarian directors are left, academic librarians are now involved to some degree in decision making in almost every academic library. In particular, the committee system has been found to be a feasible method of providing employees' input. Academic libraries often have committees on public services, technical processing, personnel, and automation whose membership might include people from various library departments and with various staff ratings (Marchant 1982, p. 783). A few small libraries have adopted the faculty model of collegial governance with a rotating chair and with most decisions being made by a committee comprised of all librarians (Bechtel 1981), but the sheer size of most academic libraries has made the collegial model an impractical one to follow.

Although most academic libraries retain a pyramidal structure, they have also

> *. . .established or invigorated some kind of general or representative assembly for deliberation and determination of*

large issues, strategic long-range plans, goals and objectives, and self-governance. The pyramid appears to remain largely intact but with a much clearer ambient understanding...of its true function and virtue as a device for implementing decisions made not within it but elsewhere (Kaser 1977, p. 68).

The amount of participation permitted will vary from library to library, but the issues facing academic libraries are so complex and the need for specialized expertise so great that the trend toward shared decision making will continue in academic libraries.

Preparation of Academic Librarians

Today's academic librarians are better educated than ever before. More have master's degrees in librarianship, more have or are studying for additional degrees, and more are engaged in continuing education, institutes, and workshops (Stone 1982, p. 39). Individual librarian's professional development and professional contribution have been emphasized. These developments in the library profession must continue—and expand—to ensure that tomorrow's librarians will be able to handle the fundamental and far-reaching changes in providing scholarly information to academic institutions. "The quality of the library staff during the next decade will be more important to the future health and vitality of the university than the quality of the instructional and administrative staff" (Battin 1983, p. 22). Academic libraries need to be able to attract the best and the brightest to their staffs.

The qualifications required of a person entering the field of academic librarianship have been much discussed in the profession of late. Four qualifications are critical: (1) a first-rate mind with the ability to solve problems; (2) a solid undergraduate preparation in any of a variety of disciplines (the key is the rigor of the training); (3) concrete evidence of managerial abilities because almost every research library responsibility, even at the entry level, now requires some degree of sophisticated management of either people or resources; and (4) an intellectual commitment to research librarianship (Battin 1983, p. 23).

The personnel directors of a group of large academic research libraries were polled to clarify the requirements in addition to a master's degree in library science that those libraries had established for beginning librarians. The respondents wanted entry-level librarians to have previous library experience and skills in foreign language(s), and they preferred candidates with a second master's degree. In addition to bibliographic skills, these personnel officers wanted candidates skilled in management, automation/computer networking, online reference and cataloging, and research (Creth and Harders 1980, p. 2169). A similar study of the directors of large research libraries found that in addition to the more traditional bibliographic competencies, a variety of skills in analysis, human relations, and computer application and retrieval were desirable (Marchant and Smith 1982).

Schools of library science have responded to these demands and have adjusted their curricula to meet the needs of academic libraries. Although no schools prepare students exclusively to work for academic libraries, most schools offer students a chance to specialize in academic or research libraries. Library school curricula now reflect the advent of technology, and most new graduates have had courses in automation, programming, and online searching and cataloging. Many schools also permit or require their students to take a "field experience" or "practicum" to give them some practical experience in an academic library before they assume their first job. A growing number of schools are requiring courses in research methods. And to add the new skills needed by librarians without sacrificing any of the traditional bibliographic skills, a few schools have expanded the length of their master's program from 36 to 48 semester hours (Stueart 1982).

Some librarians have also realized that it is impossible to expect a student to acquire all the competencies that have been labeled as essential for a beginning librarian in the typical 36-hour program. A few attempts have been made to establish internships for new library school graduates to provide a bridge between library school and a permanent position in a library. The University of Michigan library has developed a residency program that "will be structured to provide residents not only with a practical working situation, but with specialized instruction on skills and issues central to the practice of research librarianship" (Dougherty and Lougee 1983, p. 1324).

Academic administrators must become aware that to attract and keep the best individuals in academic librarianship, higher salaries will be required. Academic libraries are competing with private industries for librarians and information scientists, and, in many instances, academic libraries are losing the competition. Many of the best library school students are

To attract and keep the best individuals in academic librarianship, higher salaries will be required.

being hired by special libraries (especially corporate libraries), which are also luring away some of the most competent librarians already working in academic libraries. This situation is at least partially the result of the differences in salaries between academe and the private sector (Abell and Coolman 1982, pp. 81–82). The beginning master's degree librarian hired by an academic library in 1983 was paid an average annual salary of $16,617 (Learmont and Van Houten 1984, p. 1811). In comparison, graduates of the University of Pittsburgh with a bachelor's degree in information science reported an average starting salary in 1981 of $19,217 for their jobs as programmers, systems analysts, market research associates, and manufacturing engineers (Abell and Coolman 1982, p. 82). To recruit and retain individual librarians trained at the highest level, academic institutions must be prepared to offer salaries that are competitive with those offered by the private sector. At the same time, it cannot be forgotten that salaries of support staff should also be reexamined regularly to make certain that they are comparable with nonlibrary positions requiring similar qualifications and making similar demands.

In addition to establishing attractive pay scales, administrators must also provide a challenging work environment for new library school graduates and foster an experience that offers variety and depth instead of routine, limited activities. To avoid future job dissatisfaction, attention must be paid to the working conditions of experienced librarians. Ways must be found to alleviate the perceptions some individuals have of being trapped in one job forever. Job rotation, shared positions, and flex-time may all help increase job satisfaction (Stueart 1984, p. 1725). Some libraries have instituted two-track personnel systems to encourage the retention of and improve the morale of more experienced staff members. This type of system allows librarians to advance in salary and in professional rank through either the administrative or the "professional" track, thus recognizing the varied ways in which an individual may contribute to the organization and the profession (Taylor 1984, p. 202).

Even librarians who enter academic libraries with the best educational preparation will need continual updating to stay current. "A rapidly changing age is forcing all libraries and all individuals who work in them to attach a new importance to personnel development and continuing education (Stone 1971, p. 16). Fortunately, a variety of workshops and institutes are available to provide continuing education. A practitioner can seek continuing education as an individual, and in many academic libraries, continuing education programs are being brought to the library so that staff members can receive training at a limited cost. Human resources are too valuable for any institution to fail to invest in the training programs that the times require for upgrading staff. Some librarians may need extensive retraining to prepare them to work with computers or to prepare them for new positions in other parts of the library. The fear of automation could at least be partially alleviated if librarians knew that some systematic plans were being made to retrain any individuals who would be replaced by automation.

Given the radical and rapid pace of change in the conditions and demands that academic librarians confront, it is essential that thoughtful and rigorous programs be developed to help these active professionals maintain effective and relevant skills (Abell and Coolman 1982, p. 81).

If in the future the academic library becomes decentralized as some suggest (Atkinson 1984; Cline and Sinnott 1983; Martell 1983), the demands on the academic librarian will become more intense. Instead of being a specialist in cataloging, reference, or collection development, a librarian might be assigned to work in a specific subject area and have overall responsibility for collection management and use, including providing reference services to the scholars using the portion of the collection for which he or she is responsible. Librarians would become subject specialists in particular areas, and it would be unlikely for a librarian to work in more than one subject field in the course of a career (Cline and Sinnott 1983, p. 175).

In this decentralized organization, it would be imperative for every librarian to know not only all facets of librarianship but also to know in depth the subject area in which he or she worked. The second master's degree that is now being increasingly required for academic librarians would probably become mandatory, and it would not be surprising if many more librarians obtained doctorates in their subject area. Librarians would be transformed from information generalists who know a little about many areas into information specialists who know a lot about one field of study. If this organizational pattern comes into being, the demands upon librarians will be greater, but at the same time this reorganization might provide a solution to the problem of the academic librarian's low status on campus. In a decentralized and individualized structure, librarians would work directly with faculty and students to provide the information they need. One can assume that the contributions academic librarians make to the educational process would be clear and that the respect and the status academic librarians have desired would subsequently be realized.

Other Personnel Issues

Two other topics have occupied the attention of librarians over the last 20 years.

The first is the position of women in academic libraries. Librarianship is a profession that is dominated by females: More than 80 percent of all librarians are women. Academic librarianship has a higher proportion of males than any other type of librarianship, but still approximately 65 percent of academic librarians are women. Within academic librarianship, as within the rest of the profession, a dual career structure has existed: Men hold the leadership roles and women fill subordinate positions. Far fewer women than men are appointed library directors, and those that are have usually been found in small, private liberal arts colleges. "The power, the prestige, and the largest salaries within the field go to the minority of practitioners, who are male" (Heim 1983, p. 1). Studies have shown that females' lower status cannot be attributed to lack of mobility (Braunagel 1979) or to lack of professional qualifications (Moran 1983) and that women have found it harder to obtain directorships when they are external candidates (Metz 1978).

Within recent years, the position of women in academic librarianship has seemed to improve somewhat. The large ARL libraries, whose directorships were a few years ago held entirely by men, now have 16 female directors (Phenix 1984, p. 290). Many women directors serve in middle-size and small college libraries. In addition, a group of competent and talented women hold positions as associate directors and departmental heads and will soon be ready to move into higher administrative positions. To date, no research has proved conclusively that the position of women in academic libraries is getting better—the evidence is largely anecdotal and scattered—and further research is needed to show whether women are finally moving into top administrative positions in proportion to their number in the profession. Some fear that the Reagan administration's lack of support for affirmative action may slow the progress that women have made in academic libraries.

The second issue is unionization. As in the rest of higher education, the arrival of collective bargaining in academic libraries has been viewed with ambivalence. In most cases where librarians have unionized, they have formed part of the faculty bargaining unit, but librarians have often felt that their concerns were overlooked in bargaining.

> *The special goals of minorities have to be pretty inexpensive to prevail in this system. Academic librarians are a perennial minority, between four and ten percent of the unit, and must expect considerable frustration as a result* (Weatherford 1976, p. 112).

In a later study, Weatherford (1980) listed the distinctions made between faculty and librarians in bargaining agreements — distinctions in salary, workload, and tenure that were to the disadvantage of the librarians.

To date unionization has brought mixed results. On the plus side, unions have contributed to the formalization of personnel policies and procedures, improved communications, increased fringe benefits, and improved working conditions. On the negative side, they have caused substantially more paperwork, contributed to the establishment of more rigid work rules, and created an adversary relationship between librarians and managers (Stone 1982, p. 37). To date not enough research has been done about the effects of unionization on academic libraries. Unionization is a complex issue, and because of its importance and its possible effects on the library profession, facts are needed to document and implement future planning (Stone 1982, p. 47).

The emphasis in libraries is shifting from collections to access. Providing access to information will be the principal goal and activity. . .of the emerging information age library. Those who use libraries, and those who provide their financial support, must recognize and accept this new reality. The explosion in the quantity, cost, and communicability of information is a new phenomenon [that] calls for new responses. . . . It should be clear to all by now that no research library can meet its users' needs solely, or even largely, from its own book, journal, and manuscript collections (De Gennaro 1984b, p. 1205).

In the decades following World War II, higher education in the United States experienced an unprecedented period of prosperity and growth. Academic libraries eagerly took advantage of the available funds and invested heavily in library materials. Not surprisingly, one of the most significant developments to take place in academic libraries during that period was the phenomenal growth of library collections.

This growth was most evident in the large research universities. In 1963, 11 members of the Association of Research Libraries owned collections of 1 million volumes; by 1983, 104 owned collections of 1 million and eight had more than 5 million volumes. Harvard, the largest, grew from a collection of 4.8 million volumes to a total of 10.6 million in 1983 (Molyneux 1984).

The collections of smaller institutions were also strengthened. The expenditures from appropriations, gifts, and grants improved basic collections, reference collections, and journal holdings (Holley 1977, p. 25). A great gap is apparent, however, between the collections of the large university libraries and the smaller college libraries. Although some well-established liberal arts colleges and some publicly supported comprehensive colleges have strong collections, many others, especially private liberal arts colleges, have libraries that do not meet the Association of College and Research Libraries' *Standards for College Libraries* in terms of size and growth of the collection, staff, and budgets. "In sum, for most [college] libraries it seems fair to say that they are underdeveloped, understaffed, and underused. Assuming that the *Standards* are reasonable, far greater support for all library functions is required for the great majority of libraries" (Carpenter 1981, p. 18). Although the holdings of college libraries improved after World War II, most of them began from a very small base and never had the funds to develop a substantial collection. Of the more than 2,500 institutions of higher education, very few institutions have multimillion volume collections. It is, however, in this minority of institutions that most advanced research takes place (Fussler 1973, p. 34).

The Development of Collections in Academic Libraries

During the post–World War II era, academic libraries placed enormous emphasis on developing collections. "Collection development" is a term used to describe how the library's resources are expended in purchasing library materials – that is, which books, serials, and other items should be added to the library's collection. This activity involves a continuous series of choices made within the context of the library's policy based upon an understanding of local academic needs, priorities, and goals. Those responsible for collection development in a library must be familiar with the processes of scholarship, especially scholarly communication (Osburn 1982, p. 46). Collection development usually involves the combined efforts of library staff, administration, and faculty. Most large academic libraries have collection development officers who coordinate the activity, using the talents of bibliographers to select materials from specified subject areas.

The growth of libraries after World War II reflected the results of this collection development. Collections were constantly expanded. Many distinguished collections were amassed in that period, and collection building and growth were the overriding concerns of most librarians. Libraries were ranked by the size of their collections, and bigger was always better (Holley 1984).

The days of rapid expansion of library collections came to an end in the 1970s with the general downturn in the financing of higher education. Collection development no longer involved selecting all the most important scholarly works published; instead it became a process of deciding from among that list which titles the library had funds to acquire.

Library budgets began to stagnate just at the time that the prices of books and journals began to escalate at an unprecedented rate, resulting in the severe erosion of purchasing power. In fact, library acquisition budgets were hit harder than most aspects of university budgets because the price of books and journals rose more rapidly than any other cost of higher education, except energy (Osburn 1982, p. 50). Halstead's (1983) *Inflation Measures for Schools and Colleges* documents this rapid increase. U.S. hardcover books rose from a base of 100 in fiscal year 1967 to 375.4 in 1982, foreign monographs increased to 487.5, and U.S. periodicals rose to 509. In other words, U.S. books are 3½ times more expensive, foreign monographs nearly five times more expensive, and periodicals over five times more expensive than they were in 1967. During the same period, general inflation, as measured by the Consumer Price Index, rose to 263.1.

Not only were prices increasing for library materials; at the same time, the amount of material being published increased. The "information explosion" that began after World War II continued unabated. The number of books and journals being published mushroomed. As fields of study grew and subdivided, they produced numerous new journals, and few of the old ones ceased publication. The number of monograph titles published annually, both in the United States and in other nations, grew rapidly. In the United States, hardcover monographs increased 14 percent per year during the 1960s and 2.8 percent per year in the 1970s. In the rest of the world, the publication of monographs increased 4 percent per year in the 1960s and 4.4 percent per year during the 1970s (Harvey and Spyers-Duran 1984, p. 22).

The increases in the rate of growth in journal publications not only exceeded the rate of growth for monographic publications, but inflation also affected the cost of journals more than books. The cost of scientific and technical journals, whose base price was higher than other journals to start, rose fastest of all.

In many university libraries this situation was reflected in the acquisition budgets by a growing proportion of the budget being occupied by serials (subscription publications) and by a growing proportion of the serials expenditures being occupied by science and technology journals. It became clear that the extreme logical conclusion of this trend would be that our libraries would eventually find affordable no books at all and only one journal, a chemistry journal (Osburn 1982, p. 50).

As a larger proportion of acquisition budgets was used for the purchase of periodicals, academic libraries began to fall behind on purchases of monographs. In ARL libraries, the number of volumes added in 1970 averaged 102,171, but by 1981 the average number added had dropped to 78,241. The statistics for smaller universities and colleges show a similar pattern of decline (Harvey and Spyers-Duran 1984, pp. 23–24). Despite the increased proportion of the acquisition budget devoted to serials, academic libraries were not able to stay abreast of the increases in costs, and libraries not only began to decide not to place new subscription orders and to cancel duplicates but also to report heavy cancellation of single and unique titles (National Enquiry 1979, p. 137).

Although the rate of yearly increases in cost have subsided somewhat, the prices that libraries must pay for periodicals are higher than many library users would ever expect. The average subscription price for an American periodical in 1984 was $54.97, a 9.4 percent increase over the average price of a subscription in 1983. Subdivided by category, average subscription prices range from a low of $12.21 for a children's periodical to a high of $228.90 for a chemistry or physics periodical (Brown and Phillips 1984, p. 1422). The costs of indexing and abstracting tools to allow access to periodicals has also increased. For instance, the average cost of one of the common Wilson indexes *(Reader's Guide, Business Periodicals Index, Applied Science and Technology Index)* is now $651.50 a year (Brown and Phillips 1984, p. 1425). Reflecting the typically higher costs of scientific and technical materials, an academic library's subscription to *Chemistry Abstracts* cost $6,400 per year in 1984. The annual cost to degree-granting institutions for the same subscription in 1985 will be $7,200.

Books are comparably expensive. The average price of a hardcover book in 1983 was $30.84. Again, average prices vary widely, from a low of $9.69 for a juvenile book to a high of $46.97 for a sociology or economics book (Grannis 1984, p. 415). Because few academic libraries purchase children's periodicals or children's books and because many of their acquisitions are in the high-cost categories, their average cost per subscription or volume is likely higher than the examples cited. In addition, the prices cited do not include the total cost to the library of adding a new subscription or a new book because they exclude the costs associated with processing the item to get it ready for the library shelf and the cost of storage, building maintenance, and use—the relatively invisible costs of acquisition.

Academic libraries have reluctantly realized that their previous levels of collection development could no longer be maintained. Each year a smaller percentage of the world's published output is added to library collections. Libraries are turning to new methods to help them shape their collections under these new circumstances. Many libraries are turning to collection use studies and citation analyses as means of gathering information about what portions of the collection are being most heavily used (Axford 1981; Kent et al. 1979; Shaw 1978). As colleges and universities find it harder to finance new library buildings and as libraries begin to run out of storage space in the old ones, interest is increasing in the no-growth or steady-state library (Gore 1976). Libraries are trying to develop their collections more systematically, using tools such as the Collection Analysis Plan developed in 1977 by ARL's Office of Management Studies to enable librarians to analyze collection, acquisition, retention, resource sharing, and preservation (Bentz and Hanlin 1982, p. 136).

Libraries have been forced to devote their funds to their most needed acquisitions and have been able to pay little attention to the research needs of tomorrow.

> *The effort to meet the immediate daily needs of scholarship has detracted from those of anticipating future scholarly needs and developing the ideally well-rounded collection. This shift in emphasis has manifested itself in decreased acquisition of older, yet significant, materials as a means to preserve the established acquisition level of current publications. The effects of this change on the development of scholarly resources are considerable, with generally more immediate and specific negative implications for the kinds of scholarship requiring historical perspective* (Osburn 1982, p. 50).

Specialists in collection development have long stressed the importance of collecting now for the research needs of tomorrow, because it is often impossible to acquire the materials retrospectively. "Building collections to satisfy current demand is building them too late, and librarians must instead anticipate the research interests of twenty years hence" (Handlin 1984, p. 217).

Academic librarians have faced up to the fact that no library—no matter how large—can be self-sufficient and collect all the materials that researchers who use it would like to have. The days of the comprehensive, self-contained collection are over. If librarians are going to be able to meet the needs of users, today and tomorrow, they will have to rely on resource sharing as an integral part of their activities.

Sharing Resources

After studying the future needs of scholars and researchers, the National Enquiry into Scholarly Communication (1979) recommended the establishment of a national bibliographic system that would permit scholars to identify information pertinent to their work and would indicate how and where that information could be obtained. Although numerous bibliographic databases have been created in recent years,

> the task ahead is to build upon these efforts by linking them together into an accessible bibliographic system that will serve the members of the research community, regardless of a scholar's field of study or location. Such a system will also help in the internal operations of libraries, making it possible to improve their performance (National Enquiry 1979, p. 16).

While America's academic libraries are not yet linked in a comprehensive national bibliographic system, they have made great strides in their collaborative efforts.

Interests in cooperative schemes for collection development is not new in academic libraries. The Farmington Plan, begun in 1948, was an effort to make sure that at least one copy of each new foreign title that might be useful to research in the United States was acquired by an American library. A government-funded program was begun in 1962 that permitted surplus American-owned unconvertible foreign currency to be spent in its country of origin to buy books and library materials, which were then deposited in libraries specializing in collections of materials from the area. In 1960, some 35 American research libraries with a strong interest in South America began a cooperative venture, the Latin American Co-Operative Acquisitions Program. For various reasons, all of these early cooperative ventures were severely cut back or ceased to exist in the more straitened financial climate of the 1970s.

Other more successful ventures remain in existence. Many academic libraries, especially those geographically close, began cooperative plans of acquisitions and storage. One example of such a consortium is the Hampshire Inter-Library Center established in 1951, whose members, Amherst, Hampshire, Mount Holyoke, and Smith Colleges and the University of Massachusetts, cooperate in a number of resource-sharing plans (Edmonds and Bridegam 1979). Another example is the arrangement at Duke University and the University of North

Carolina at Chapel Hill, which have for many years engaged in cooperative acquisition programs in certain subject areas (Osburn 1979, p. 139).

A cooperative undertaking on a larger scale is the Center for Research Libraries (CRL) in Chicago. The center was established in 1949 by 10 midwestern institutions, which deposited collections of their little-used materials in the center. Only one copy of each title was kept in storage. The center thus provided access for its members to infrequently used materials, while the remote storage of those holdings released much-needed space in the member libraries. The center's membership has grown from 10 to well over 100 members. CRL now has over 3.5 million items in its collection (Glicksman 1984). The center not only stores donated items but also buys, at shared expense, materials that it anticipates will be necessary but whose use would not warrant acquisition by individual libraries—for example, foreign newspapers, scientific and technical publications in foreign languages, and foreign doctoral dissertations. Member libraries are provided rapid access to the materials in storage as the primary purpose of the operation is to serve as a resource sharing center. The CRL has played an increasingly important role in supplying needed periodicals by relying on the British Library Lending Division at Boston Spa, England, to fill requests when the center does not own the requested materials (Simpson 1983).

It is not surprising that the use of the CRL to provide access to periodicals has been expanding. Gaining access to periodicals is one of the most severe problems academic libraries, especially research libraries, face. The establishment of a periodical center that would provide access to journal and other periodical literature has been much discussed in recent years. A model exists in Great Britain in the government-funded British Library Lending Division, founded in 1961, which now provides libraries in Great Britain and abroad with access to all types of periodicals. The British Lending Library is often considered "the most useful and efficient dedicated collection in the world—tangible evidence that centralized sharing can work" (Biggs 1984, p. 4). American librarians hoped to be able to institute a comparable facility in the United States. Because of the high cost associated with establishing and operating such a facility, however, substantial federal funding would be required.

Advocates of a national periodical center do not agree entirely on the type of center needed nor on the functions it

Gaining access to periodicals is one of the most severe problems academic libraries, especially research libraries, face.

should perform, but they generally accept the following objectives:

> *[A national periodical center] should provide a faster, cheaper, more fully reliable access to periodical literature in such a way as to facilitate the more rational allocation of local library funds and to lighten the load on heavy net lenders. Periodicals in all languages, on all subjects except medicine, and of all degrees of use should be collected....* *Center operations should be flexible enough to exploit new technology as it [becomes] available and cost effective* (Biggs 1984, p. 4).

The center is not intended to serve only as a storehouse for periodical material. Instead, a more active role has been proposed in which the center would serve as a distribution agent for publishers of certain types of materials. The center would ensure that all copied materials comply fully with the copyright law. The establishment of the center opens new possibilities for alternative types of publications, such as on-demand publishing (National Enquiry 1979, pp. 18–19).

After a series of studies, the House of Representatives passed legislation establishing the National Periodical Center in 1979. The bill then stalled in the Senate and was never passed. The legislation failed for several reasons: the opposition of publishers who feared its creation would cause libraries to drop subscriptions, a belief that new technology would render the center obsolete, and deep divisions of opinion within the library community (Biggs 1984). "It now seems unlikely that the Center will ever be established in anything like its originally envisioned form—or indeed in any form [that] will substantially relieve the pressures on libraries" (p. 2).

In 1973, Herman Fussler had advocated the establishment of a national "pool" for the comprehensive acquisition of current serial and monographic resources, arguing that this centralized approach is the most efficient and cost-effective means of sharing resources. He also pointed out, however, that another approach to resource sharing "would be based upon the division of acquisition responsibilities among existing libraries by designating subject fields or other categories and a reliance upon an improved system of interlibrary loan for access" (pp. 76–77). He saw this system of access as more costly, less reliable, less comprehensive, and slower than access through a centralized pool. The failure to establish the National Periodicals Center seems to indicate that libraries will have to rely on a more decentralized approach to resource sharing. The development of new computerized methods of bibliographic access and the advent of new methods of text transmission since Fussler wrote may serve to alleviate some of the disadvantages he saw associated with decentralization.

Libraries have always relied heavily on one decentralized system of resource sharing – interlibrary loan (ILL). At one time, it was difficult to know what library owned the specific item needed to fulfill a patron's request. Most requests were routinely sent to the nearest large research library believed most likely to have the needed item. This approach led to a few large libraries' lending many more volumes than they borrowed, but to some extent this inequity has been partially corrected by the use of the bibliographic utilities. Although developed primarily for use in cataloging, these utilities also permit users to know what libraries hold what titles by looking up a specific item in the online bibliographic database. With the bibliographic utilities, requests for ILL can be transmitted directly by computer or by more traditional means like mail or teletype to the nearest library known to own the item. Without a doubt, the use of bibliographic databases has assisted in the equalization of interlibrary loan requests, but the larger libraries are still usually net lenders and the smaller ones net borrowers. Like everything else in libraries, interlibrary loans are not inexpensive: The average interlibrary loan transaction now costs between $7 and $14. These high costs have forced libraries to look more closely at the question of financing ILL.

A great outcry has been raised against fees for service as a barrier to freedom of access to information. But the issue has been confused with the question of how society pays for these services because they do not come free. It costs money to develop bibliographic tools, and to acquire, store, locate, and deliver bibliographic materials. The question is not whether we pay for them but who pays, how to pay, and how to distribute the payments equitably. In order for resource sharing to work it is essential to develop effective methods of cost sharing, whether these costs are borne by government agencies, librarians, or individuals (Kronick 1982, p. 135).

Many libraries are now charging for ILL, but no uniform fee schedule and no consensus exist about whether the fees should be absorbed by the library or passed along to the patron. To ensure that interlibrary loan will function better in the future than it did in the past, an equitable and uniform system of reimbursing the lending library must be devised. Some states have developed statewide interlibrary loan systems, but much work still needs to be done in this area.

Another more systematic approach to sharing resources through shared collection development can be seen in the activities of the Research Libraries Group (RLG), which was established by Columbia, Yale, The New York Public Library, and Harvard in 1974 to achieve planned, coordinated cooperation. By the end of 1982, RLG had 26 full, affiliate, and associate members and 16 special members of the partnership (Gwinn and Mosher 1983, p. 128). RLG operates RLIN, a bibliographic utility, and its other principal programs include collection management and development, shared resources, and preservation. RLG has developed a method to coordinate collection development among its members by the use of the RLG Conspectus. The Conspectus summarizes RLG members' collection strengths by subject.

> *The invention of the RLG Conspectus derived from the fortuitous conjunction of individuals sharing common interests and goals, the expansion of RLG membership, and agreement that something like a national collection development policy would be necessary to protect the research capacity of the nation's universities from the impact of repeated and unfavorable economic cycles. Using this tool, research libraries could focus collective resources on appropriate distributed but coordinated effort, thus ensuring availability of unique or rare titles to the nation's scholars* (Gwinn and Mosher 1983, p. 129).

The RLG Conspectus is available online and can be searched by subject, class, collection level, and institution. A bibliographer trying to decide whether or not to buy an expensive item could check the Conspectus to see whether another library has ordered the item or to see what institutions have a comprehensive collection and a commitment to continue to add to that collection in the subject area. Information garnered from the search would permit the bibliographer to make a more informed judgment about the necessity to add the item to the library's collection. RLG hopes that the Conspectus can "become the cornerstone of a larger national cooperative effort...among all of the principal research libraries of the nation for the eventual benefit of generations of scholars" (Gwinn and Mosher 1983, p. 129).

Resource sharing, especially resource sharing through formalized networks, seems the most promising method of ensuring that academic libraries can stay abreast of the needs of scholars and researchers in this country. It is clearly too expensive to rely on local collections alone. The emphasis in academic libraries is now shifting from collections to access (De Gennaro 1984b, p. 1205). Libraries are moving away from their past emphasis on collection building and growth to a new emphasis on providing access to information from many sources.

Libraries will clearly have to continue to supply their users' routine needs, however. Resource sharing will be more necessary in large research universities, where the demand for little-used and more esoteric materials will be greater. Small and medium-sized libraries will still need to devote the bulk of their resources to collection development because "each institution will continue to be responsible for the provision of undergraduate requirements. No network now envisaged will enable institutions to shift to others the cost of providing instructional material" (Munn 1983, p. 352). But small libraries may also need to share resources, because the economic and technological factors that have combined to make resource sharing inevitable for research libraries are having the same effects on small academic libraries (Holicky 1984). Small and medium-sized libraries will definitely rely on resource sharing to some extent; they have traditionally used interlibrary loan to fill requests for items the library does not own. Nevertheless, large university libraries used by numerous researchers, faculty, and doctoral students will generate the most requests for special or peripheral research material, which will have to be met from external sources.

Library users greet the concept of resource sharing with less than great enthusiasm, even when they intellectually accept the premise that no library can be autonomous in meeting a broad spectrum of research needs. "Many scholars and other users are probably distrustful of any plan that locates in a remote institution any significant portion of the resources required, or potentially required, by an investigator or student" (Fussler 1973, p. 33). Access to materials through resource sharing is considerably less convenient than access through a local collection. To date, interlibrary loan has too often been a slow, cumbersome, and uncertain method of obtaining needed materials. Fortunately, however, the structuring of networks, the use of technology, and the promise of new methods of document delivery should improve the mechanisms for sharing. New digital telefacsimile equipment has the potential to be a rapid and economical means for interlibrary lending (Boss 1984, p. 1188). In addition, methods of document delivery such as microwaves, satellites, and cable television with local print-out capacity hold promise for quicker document delivery in the future. As the concept of the library changes from a warehouse for books to a center for access to information from a variety of sources, library networking and resource sharing will offer a powerful tool to administrators seeking to maximize the research resources for their institution (Shaw 1982, p. 60).

New Formats in Library Collections

Technology has had a major effect on the types of materials now found in library collections. Academic library collections are no longer collections comprised almost entirely of books but collections comprised of materials in multiple formats.

The first new format academic libraries collected widely was the 35mm microfilm, which began to appear in library collections in the 1930s (Webb 1977, p. 143). Various other microforms—microcards, microfiche, and ultrafiche—have since appeared. Many academic libraries expanded their collections greatly by adding microforms, and a great number of important monographs, journals, government publications, manuscripts, and archives that were previously available only in original formats became widely accessible (Bentz and Hanlin 1982, p. 125). The great advantage of microforms is that they can be stored in a much smaller space than would be required by a paper copy of the same work. They also are usually cheaper than a paper copy and can be used to add items to the collection that would otherwise not be available. The greatest disadvantage of microforms has always been that many library users dislike reading materials in this format. The introduction of more sophisticated, less bulky equipment that provides easier viewing has made microforms more acceptable now than they were in the past, however.

During the 1950s and 1960s, many academic libraries added a large number of audiovisual materials to their collections. Films, filmstrips, records, and audiotapes were widely accepted in academic libraries, especially for use in undergraduate instruction. Videotapes and videodiscs became part of many audiovisual collections in the 1970s.

The section of this monograph concerned with technology in academic libraries has already dealt with the new importance of online databases in libraries. Online bibliographic and textual databases have become quite common in many libraries. Some libraries are also considering providing access to aggregate data, such as voting records, census data, and economic statistics. As researchers will need both the data and the facility to manipulate them, libraries providing this aggregate data must furnish both the data and the statistical programs necessary to manipulate them. Although libraries may not store either the data or statistical programs, they "will provide the nexus and computers to which the data are transmitted from a regional or national database" (Atkinson and Stenstrom 1984, p. 283).

Most librarians are already collecting materials in multiple formats, and the future promises to bring even more variety to the library. Certain segments of the publishing industry are changing greatly, and these changes will affect both the way information is packaged and the way it is distributed.

One of the alarming changes occurring in publishing is the movement of traditional commercial publishers and corporate giants like AT&T and IBM into the "knowledge industry" on a fee-for-use basis.

Our entire structure of higher education and scholarly endeavor has been built upon a communication process for scholars subsidized by universities through their academic libraries.... [W]e are now in a situation where our scholars generate information in the universities, give it away to the publishers (or in some instances pay to have it published), and then our libraries buy it back at increasingly prohibitive cost (Battin 1982a, p. 581).

Because information technology now offers the opportunity to provide access to material on a fee-for-use basis, if librarians and publishers do not work together and transcend their disagreements, then universities and libraries will be bypassed or will become the unreimbursed marketing agents for the publisher. The ultimate result would be that the control of scholarly communication would be in the hands of the for-profit sector, which would be detrimental to the free flow of information essential for scholarship (Battin 1982a). Scholars, publishers, research libraries, and learned societies are all components of a single system and thus are fundamentally dependent on each other (National Enquiry 1979). From the viewpoint of academic librarians, it seems that some publishers are not aware of this interdependence.

The move of many publishers into electronic publishing is certain to have repercussions in the library. The demise of the library as an institution has been predicted with the advent of the "paperless society" (Lancaster 1978, 1982). When researchers have access to numerous computerized information banks, libraries "will become archives, repositories of the records of the past, serving warehouse and delivery functions but offering little service" (Lancaster 1982, p. 169).

While it is not likely that the "paperless society" will arrive before the end of the century (if then), it is certain that even more types of information will be "repackaged" in the near future and will exist in the library in electronic forms. Electronic publishing will have a major effect on libraries. Already many major reference works are available online and more will follow. It will be much faster and more economical for publishers to update information in computerized systems than it is to update and publish new editions in paper (Massman 1977, p. 154). It is probable that, because the high costs of conventional journals have resulted in many journal publishers pricing themselves out of the market, many periodicals will cease to exist in paper form and will be available only as electronic journals. If a user needs a paper copy of a portion of the journal, it could be printed on demand (Frankie 1982, p. 108). A report of a company that plans to publish 36 of these electronic journals in various scientific fields appeared recently in the *Chronicle of Higher Education* (Winkler 1982).

An interesting issue for both librarians and faculty is what effect the electronic journals will have on scholarly research. If work in progress is published, will there be danger of premature exposure of research results? Will articles be refereed? Because of the ease of publication, will there be a tendency to publish everything? How will publication in an electronic journal be equated to publication in a traditional journal when tenure and promotion are decided? Only experience with this type of publication will provide the answers.

For the foreseeable future at least, it seems likely that extensive collections of published materials will remain the heart of the academic library. Many new formats (including some not yet common, such as optical discs) will supplement the books and periodicals. As time goes on, printed sources will constitute a diminished proportion of the total information available for scholarly purposes, and as this trend progresses, librarians will deal more with "information" than with books. Although in many subject areas the archival functions of the library—the preservation of knowledge of the past—will provide users with information available in no other form, researchers in other areas may be relying entirely on electronic media.

The Preservation of Library Materials

During the last 25 years, concern has been mounting about the physical deterioration of large portions of libraries' collections. Previously, preservation was a neglected area, and today's library collections reflect that neglect (Darling and Ogden 1981, p. 9). Although scattered interest in preservation existed previously, three forces have necessitated an intensification of efforts to preserve library collections: (1) the very volume of material to be preserved is so vast that traditional preservation techniques are no longer adequate; (2) the diversity and complexity of the materials to be preserved have created different types of problems; and (3) the public is increasingly concerned about the preservation of all sorts of historical artifacts, ranging from books to historic districts (Banks 1978, p. 2). Unfortunately, the previous neglect of library collections has resulted in irreparable losses of valuable research material.

The extent of the preservation problem confronting libraries is staggering. Both the Library of Congress and Columbia University estimate, for example, that 30 percent of their collections need preservation treatment; the New York Public Library estimates that 50 percent of its collection needs such treatment (Battin 1982b, p. 65). The largest preservation problem confronting most academic libraries is "brittle books," books that were printed after the 1860s on paper that ultimately gets so brittle it cannot be handled without breaking. The paper contains so much acid that the fibers become very weak within 25 to 50 years. In any library with a large retrospective collection, a large proportion of the collection is likely to be unusable.

Compounding the problem is the fact that most libraries store books in an environment that is hostile to their preservation. A book's worst enemies are heat, light, dryness, dampness, dirt, and use. The trends in most libraries to provide brighter lighting and higher temperature for the comfort of users and to house collections in open stacks have all been detrimental to the collection. It is interesting to contrast the treatment provided for computers and for books. Computers are almost always housed in controlled environments with maximum security, while books have been provided few safeguards to prevent their deterioration. For too long library users have viewed books as sturdy and indestructible, but in reality, books, especially books exposed to heavy use and stored under adverse conditions, are very fragile (Battin 1982b, pp. 62–63).

When a book or manuscript has value as an artifact itself— for reasons such as its age, beauty, rarity, or bibliographic significance – an attempt should be made to preserve the artifact itself. Because of the great expense of preserving originals, however, for most library materials the only feasible form of preservation is through some type of reproduction. The intellectual content of the item is thus preserved, although the item itself is not (Banks 1978, pp. 2–3).

Some technical solutions are available to aid in preservation, although mass procedures for preservation are still in their infancy (Darling and Ogden 1981, p. 18). Deacidification processes have been developed to be used when preservation of the material in its original format is desired. Microfilming is a method often used when the original does not need to be kept or has deteriorated too much to be used effectively. The Library of Congress has instituted a pilot program that uses optical disk technology to preserve the intellectual content of scholarly items; the technology allows extremely high-density storage of information and offers a potentially efficient and effective means of preservation. Much current research is exploring ways to make large-scale preservation of library materials feasible (Merrill-Oldham 1984, p. 226). And publishers are being urged to use acidfree paper in the production of scholarly books.

Preservation provides a special challenge to academic libraries. Just at the time they are trying to find funds to invest in the equipment to allow them to automate library processes and to bring more computerization into the library, they are also being faced with the concurrent problem of needing to invest heavily in preservation to save their retrospective collections. Librarians cannot do the task alone, however. To date scholars or university officials have shown little interest in the massive and progressive deterioration of library collections (Battin 1982b), and again it appears the solution must be a collective one. The size of the problem and the overwhelming cost to solve it call for cooperative action.

The primary managerial challenge is to find a way, within our pluralistic society with a strong tradition of institutional individualism, to forge a coalition among the interested parties—scholars, librarians, university officers, publishers, and all who use the records of civilization—with a common purpose strong enough to transcend the barriers of apathy, tradition, myth, and institutional self-interest. Our national heritage is at stake (Battin 1982b, p. 69).

America's library collections have been built up over the years at great cost. They are truly our "national heritage," one that will be impossible to replace. Today's efforts at preservation will ensure that tomorrow's scholars can have access to these imperiled collections.

CONCLUSION

Today's academic libraries are at a crossroads. Over the next decade or two, these institutions will face fundamental changes; academic libraries of the twenty-first century are likely to be very different from those of today. The opportunities before libraries are exciting, but many obstacles must be confronted and overcome before these "about-to-be-reinvented" libraries are in place.

The library paradigm is changing, but it is "not at all [apparent] that we have a group commitment among [the library] profession as to what it should be" (Matheson 1984, p. 209). Librarians may be viewing the changes in a dangerously passive manner—expecting that new roles for librarians will evolve and that the changes taking place will be evolutionary rather than revolutionary.

> *We know that there is a total restructuring in progress of who, what, and how information is created, owned, and shared. We librarians...will be out of work, unless we... reexamine our basic assumptions and develop new strategies for staying in business* (Matheson 1984, p. 208).

New strategies must be developed if libraries are to be reformed to meet the challenges facing them during the rest of this century. The process of change is never easy, and the problems facing academic libraries will demand unprecedented attention, not only from librarians but from faculty and administrators as well. The following recommendations will help to ensure that libraries are able to make a successful transformation.

1. All libraries should be planning now for the changes that will be necessary to meet the demands of the information age.

Although some libraries are already actively engaged in planning for the future, many others have not yet begun the hard task of planning for change. All libraries need to engage in both short-term and long-term planning. This planning will be especially difficult because even present-day conditions are in flux. The technology, the publishing industry, and the amount of funding that libraries are provided are constantly changing. Nonetheless, even in the midst of the unstable present, libraries must plan the strategies to take them into the twenty-first century.

2. Both faculty and administration should assist in this planning if it is to be successful.

"We know that there is a total restructuring in progress of ...how information is created, owned, and shared."

Academic libraries cannot develop these new strategies in isolation. As components of institutions of higher education, libraries contribute to the total educational process. Too often, though, the library has been isolated from the rest of the organization. "Despite the rhetoric about it being 'the heart of the university,' the library and librarians have been for years isolated from the policy councils of most institutions.... The library has been organizationally treated as an isolated autonomous component" (Battin 1984, p. 172). Access to scholarly information is too important a topic for universities to ignore, and it has so many ramifications that it is impossible for librarians working alone to provide adequate solutions. University administrators, faculty, and librarians must work together to produce a coordinated plan to achieve the goal of providing faculty and students with the information they need for study and research. The academic community must reassess its previous concepts about libraries and develop a new consensus about what the mission of an academic library should be in the information age.

3. Universities must be willing to make the financial commitment necessary to allow libraries to retool.

This commitment will be difficult to make, because funds are limited and competing demands are numerous and important. Successful and cost-effective integration of various information support systems will require centralized long-range planning and restructured budgeting to accommodate several factors: (1) the library's archival obligations; (2) the introduction of high technology and its corollary of built-in obsolescence; (3) the magnitude of capital costs required; (4) the integration of services offered through book and journal collections, mainframes, microcomputers, and local area networks; and (5) the provision of access for local scholars to external databases and networks (Battin 1984, p. 174).

All of these services will be expensive. Libraries will not only need additional new funding; they will also need input from their parent institutions as they make policy decisions about redirecting funds away from some of the library's traditional services to new ones. Libraries and their parent institutions will also need to explore alternatives for improving libraries' efficiency. "In short, a comprehensive and imaginative effort seems required to provide the economic backdrop for the technology revolution if universities are to guide a successful library transformation in a fiscally responsible way" (Council on Library Resources 1983, p. 21).

4. Institutions of higher education should support the efforts of academic libraries to join in more cooperative ventures.

Academic libraries must participate in more cooperative ventures in support of library activities ranging from collection development to preservation. As with any cooperative effort, individual libraries will lose some of their autonomy, and library users will also face some inconvenience as libraries become less self-sufficient. It is clear, however, that academic libraries working as individual entities will not be able to solve the problems facing librarianship. Instead, the problems need to be confronted in a system that emphasizes distributed efforts and improved coordination.

These cooperative efforts will bring a change in the way libraries expend their funds. In the past, most nonpersonnel library expenditures were used for books and journals to be housed in the library for the use and benefit of that institution's students and faculty. Cooperative endeavors will force a change in this spending pattern. "Faculty and administrators must accept and support the library's growing need to spend money, not only for traditional books and journals, but also for computer systems, telecommunications, network participation, and to pay the various charges and fees that go with access to information in new ways and new forms" (De Gennaro 1984b, p. 1205).

The academic community will be forced to think less in terms of an individual library and more in terms of a national library system. We need, as the National Enquiry into Scholarly Communication suggested, to move away from the concept of self-containment to a model "in which the library will be a service center, capable of linking users to national bibliographic files and distant collections" (1979, p. 159). Paradoxically, libraries will be able to fulfill their local responsibilities only if they are able to design and develop effective cooperative systems.

It is impossible now to predict what the academic library of the twenty-first century will look like. Many models will most likely exist—ranging from some that have only begun to incorporate the new technologies into their operations to those that have used those new technologies to transform themselves into "electronic libraries" to provide information-age services to their users. It is clear that academic libraries will change—that process is well underway—but it is less clear how that change will be controlled and guided. The library as it is presently formulated may become obsolete, but the function that the academic library performs—that of providing scholarly information to the academic community—will still be central to the teaching and research of higher education. The challenge to develop and to fund the academic library of the future will be a key issue facing both higher education and librarianship as we enter the information age.

REFERENCES

The ERIC Clearinghouse on Higher Education abstracts and indexes the current literature on higher education for the National Institute of Education's monthly bibliographic journal *Resources in Education.* Most of these publications are available through the ERIC Document Reproduction Service (EDRS). For publications cited in this bibliography that are available from EDRS, ordering number and price are included. Readers who wish to order a publication should write to the ERIC Document Reproduction Service, 3900 Wheeler Avenue, Alexandria, Virginia 22304. When ordering, please specify the document number. Documents are available as noted in microfiche (MF) and paper copy (PC). Because prices are subject to change, it is advisable to check the latest issue of *Resources in Education* for current cost based on the number of pages in the publication.

Abell, Millicent D. March 1979. "The Changing Role of the Academic Librarian: Drift and Mastery." *College and Research Libraries* 40: 154–64.

Abell, Millicent D., and Coolman, Jacqueline M. 1982. "Professionalism and Productivity: Keys to the Future of Academic Library and Information Services." In *Priorities for Academic Libraries,* edited by Thomas J. Galvin and Beverly Lynch. New Directions for Higher Education No. 39. San Francisco: Jossey-Bass.

American Library Association. 1970. "Library Education and Personnel Utilization." Reprinted in *Library Management,* edited by Robert D. Stueart and John Taylor Eastlick. Littleton, Colo.: Libraries Unlimited.

Asheim, Lester. 1978. "Education of Future Academic Librarians." In *Academic Libraries by the Year 2000: Essays Honoring Jerrold Orne,* edited by Herbert Poole. New York: R.R. Bowker.

Association of Research Libraries. 1978. *Freezing Card Catalogs.* Washington, D.C.: Association of Research Libraries. ED 227 861. 83 pp. MF–$1.19; PC–$9.37.

———. 1982. *Specialty Positions in ARL Libraries.* SPEC Kit No. 80. Washington, D.C.: Association of Research Libraries, Systems and Procedures Exchange Office.

———. 1983. *Annual Report 1983.* Washington, D.C.: Association of Research Libraries, Office of Management Studies.

———. 1984. *ARL Statistics 1982–1983.* Washington, D.C.: Association of Research Libraries. ED 241 036. 73 pp. MF–$1.19; PC–$7.24.

Atkinson, Hugh C. 1984. "The Impact of New Technology on Library Organization." In *The Bowker Annual of Library and Book Trade Information,* edited by Julia Ehresmann. 29th ed. New York: R.R. Bowker.

Atkinson, Hugh C., and Stenstrom, Patricia F. 1984. "Automation in Austerity." In *Austerity Management in Academic Libraries,* edited by John F. Harvey and Peter Spyers-Duran. Metuchen, N.J.: Scarecrow Press.

Avram, Henriette D. May 1984. "Barriers: Facing the Problems." *Journal of Academic Librarianship* 10: 64–68.

Axford, H. William. January 1977. "The Three Faces of Eve: or The Identity of Academic Librarianship: A Symposium." *Journal of Academic Librarianship* 2: 276–85.

———. January 1981. "Collection Management: A New Dimension." *Journal of Academic Librarianship* 6: 324–29.

Bailey, Steven K. January 1978. "The Future of College and Research Libraries." *College and Research Libraries* 39: 4–9.

Banks, P.N. 1978. *The Preservation of Library Materials.* Chicago: Newberry Library.

Battin, Patricia. May 1980. "Research Libraries in the Network Environment: The Case for Cooperation." *Journal of Academic Librarianship* 6: 68–73.

———. April 1982a. "Libraries, Computers, and Scholarship." *Wilson Library Bulletin* 56: 580–83.

———. 1982b. "Preservation: The Forgotten Problem." In *Priorities for Academic Libraries,* edited by Thomas J. Galvin and Beverly Lynch. New Directions for Higher Education No. 39. San Francisco: Jossey-Bass.

———. January 1983. "Developing University and Research Library Professionals: A Director's Perspective." *American Libraries* 14: 22–25.

———. May 1984. "The Library: Center of a Restructured University." *College and Research Libraries* 45: 170–76.

Baumol, William J., and Blackman, S.A. 1983. "Electronics, the Cost Disease, and the Operation of Libraries." *Journal of the American Association for Information Science* 34: 181–91.

Baumol, William J., and Marcus, Matityahu. 1973. *Economics of Academic Libraries.* Washington, D.C.: American Council on Education.

Bechtel, Joan. November 1981. "Collegial Management Breeds Success." *American Libraries* 12: 605–7.

Becker, Joseph. Winter 1978. "Libraries, Society, and Technology Change." *Library Trends* 27: 409–17.

Beckman, Margaret M. November 1982. "Online Catalogs and Library Users." *Library Journal* 107: 2043–47.

———. November 1983. "Library Buildings in the Network Environment." *Journal of Academic Librarianship* 9: 281–84.

Bentz, Dale M., and Hanlin, Frank S. 1982. "Collection Development." In *Academic Librarianship: Yesterday, Today, and Tomorrow,* edited by Robert Stueart. New York: Neal-Schuman.

Biggs, Mary. Spring/Summer 1984. "The Proposed National Periodicals Center, 1973–1980: Study, Dissension, and Retreat." *Resource Sharing and Information Networks* 1: 1–22.

Boss, Richard W. June 1984. "Technology and the Modern Library." *Library Journal* 109: 1183-89.

Braunagel, Judith S. December 1979. "Job Mobility of Men and Women Librarians and How It Affects Career Advancement. *American Libraries* 10: 643-47.

Broadus, Robert N. November 1983. "Online Catalogs and Their Use." *College and Research Libraries* 44: 458-66.

Brown, Norman B., and Phillips, Jane. August 1984. "Price Indexes for 1984: U.S. Periodicals and Serial Services." *Library Journal* 109: 1422-25.

Brownrigg, Edwin B., and Lynch, Clifford A. March 1983. "Online Catalogs: Through a Glass Darkly." *Information Technology and Libraries* 2: 104-15.

Burckel, Nicholas C. January 1984. "Participatory Management in Academic Libraries: A Review." *College and Research Libraries* 45: 25-34.

Carpenter, Ray L. January 1981. "College Libraries: A Comparative Analysis in Terms of the ACRL Standards." *College and Research Libraries* 42: 7-18.

Cieslicki, Dorothy H. May 1982. "A New Status Model for Academic Libraries." *Journal of Academic Librarianship* 8: 76-81.

Cline, Hugh F., and Sinnott, Loraine T. 1983. *The Electronic Library.* Lexington, Mass.: Lexington Books.

Cohen, Jacob, and Leeson, K.W. 1979. "Sources and Uses of Funds of Academic Libraries." *Library Trends* 28: 25-45.

Council on Library Resources. 1983. *Two Reports on Research Libraries.* Washington, D.C.: Council on Library Resources. ED 238 439. 50 pp. MF-$1.19; PC-$5.49.

Creth, Sheila, and Harders, Faith. October 1980. "Requirements for the Entry-Level Librarian." *Library Journal* 105: 2168-69.

Darling, Pamela W., and Ogden, Sherelyn. 1981. "From Problems Perceived to Problems in Practice: The Preservation of Library Resources in the U.S.A., 1956-1980." *Library Resources and Technical Services* 25: 9-29.

De Gennaro, Richard. May 1975. "Austerity, Technology, and Resource Sharing: Research Libraries Face the Future." *Library Journal* 100: 917-23.

———. December 1978. "Library Administration and New Management Systems." *Library Journal* 103: 2477-82.

———. November 1979. "Research Libraries Enter the Information Age." *Library Journal* 104: 2405-10.

———. March 1981. "Matching Commitments to Needs and Resources." *The Journal of Academic Librarianship* 7: 9-13.

———. June 1982. "Libraries, Technology, and the Information Marketplace." *Library Journal* 107: 1045-54.

———. 1984a. *Into the Information Age: Report of the Director of Libraries, University of Pennsylvania, 1982-1983.* Philadelphia: University of Pennsylvania Libraries.

———. June 1984b. "Shifting Gears: Information Technology and the Academic Library." *Library Journal* 109: 1204–9.

DePew, John N. November 1983. "The ACRL Standards for Faculty Status: Panacea or Placebo." *College and Research Libraries* 44: 407–13.

Dickinson, Dennis. July 1978. "Some Reflections on Participative Management in Libraries." *College and Research Libraries* 39: 253–61.

Dickinson, Fidelia. April 1973. "Participative Management: A Left Fielder's View." *California Librarian* 34: 24–33.

Dougherty, Richard M. 1977. "Personnel Needs for Librarianship's Uncertain Future." In *Academic Libraries by the Year 2000,* edited by Herbert Poole. New York: Bowker.

Dougherty, Richard M., and Lougee, Wendy P. July 1983. "Research Library Residencies: A New Model for Professional Development." *Library Journal* 108: 1322–24.

Dowlin, Kenneth E. 1984. *The Electronic Library: The Promise and the Process.* New York: Neal-Schuman.

Droessler, Judith B., and Rholes, Julia M. November 1983. "Online Services at the Reference Desk: DIALOG, RLIN, and OCLC." *Online* 7: 79–86.

Drucker, Peter F. 1974. *Management: Tasks, Responsibilities, Practices.* New York: Harper & Row.

———. January 1976. "Managing the Public Service Institution." *College and Research Libraries* 37: 4–14.

Dunlap, Connie R. September 1976. "Organizational Patterns in Academic Libraries, 1876–1976." *College and Research Libraries* 37: 395–407.

Edelman, Henrick, and Tatum, G. Marvin. May 1976. "The Development of Collections in American University Libraries." *College and Research Libraries* 37: 222–45.

Edmonds, Anne C., and Bridegam, Willis E. 1979. "Perspectives on Cooperation: The Evaluation of a Consortium." In *New Horizons for Academic Libraries,* edited by Robert D. Stueart and Richard D. Johnson. New York: K.G. Saur.

English, Thomas G. May 1983. "Librarian Status in the Eighty-nine U.S. Academic Institutions of the Association of Research Libraries: 1982." *College and Research Libraries* 44: 199–211.

Farmer, Sharon Cline. September 1982. "RLIN as a Reference Tool." *Online* 6: 14–22.

Fayen, Emily Gallup. 1983. *The Online Catalog: Improving Public Access to Library Materials.* White Plains, N.Y.: Knowledge Industry Publications.

Ferguson, Douglas; Kaske, Neal K.; Lawrence, Gary S.; Matthews, Joseph R.; and Zich, Robert. June 1982. "The CRL Public Online Catalog Study: An Overview." *Information Technology and Libraries* 1: 84–88.

Fine, Beth Phillips. 1984. "Higher Education Act, Title II-A, College Library Resources." In *The Bowker Annual of Library and Book Trade Information,* edited by Julia Ehresmann. 29th ed. New York: R.R. Bowker.

Fine, Sarah. 1980. "Technology and Libraries: A Behavioral Perspective." In *Communicating Information: Proceedings of the 43rd ASIS Annual Meeting,* edited by Alan R. Benenfeld and Edward John Kazlauskas. White Plains, N.Y.: Knowledge Industry Publications.

Frankie, Suzanne O. October 1982. "Collection Development in Academic Libraries." *Catholic Library World* 54: 103–9.

Freedman, Maurice J. June 1984. "Automation and the Future of Technical Services." *Library Journal* 109: 1197–1203.

Fussler, Herman H. 1973. *Research Libraries and Technology: A Report to the Sloan Foundation.* Chicago: University of Chicago Press.

Galvin, Thomas J., and Lynch, Beverly P., eds. 1982. *Priorities for Academic Libraries.* New Directions for Higher Education No. 39. San Francisco: Jossey-Bass.

Gapen, D. Kaye. 1979. "Cataloging: Workflow and Productivity." In *OCLC: A National Library Network,* edited by Anne Marie Allison and Ann Allan. Short Hills, N.J.: Enslow.

Glicksman, Maurice. July 1984. "Some Thoughts on the Future of the Center for Research Libraries." *The Journal of Academic Librarianship* 10: 148–50.

Goodwin, C. A. 1974. *The Library of Congress.* New York: Praeger.

Gore, Daniel. 1976. "Farewell to Alexandria: The Theory of the No-Growth, High-Performance Library." In *Farewell to Alexandria,* edited by Daniel Gore. Westport, Conn.: Greenwood.

Gorman, Michael. July/August 1979. "On Doing Away with Technical Service Departments." *American Libraries* 10: 435–37.

Govan, James F. Fall 1977. "The Better Mousetrap: External Accountability and Staff Participation." *Library Trends* 26: 255–67.

Grannis, Chandler B. 1984. "Book Title Output and Average Prices: 1983 Preliminary Figures." In *The Bowker Annual of Library and Book Trade Information,* edited by Julia Ehresmann. 29th ed. New York: R.R. Bowker.

Guskin, Alan E.; Stoffle, Carla J.; and Baruth, Barbara E. May 1984. "Library Future Shock: The Microcomputer and the New Role of the Library." *College and Research Libraries* 45: 177–83.

Gwinn, Nancy E., and Mosher, Paul H. March 1983. "Coordinating Collection Development: The RLG Conspectus." *College and Research Libraries* 44: 128–40.

Halstead, D. Kent. 1983. *Inflation Measures for Schools and Colleges.* Washington, D.C.: U.S. Government Printing Office.

Hamlin, Arthur T. 1981. *The University Library in the United States.* Philadelphia: University of Pennsylvania Press.

Handlin, Oscar. May 1984. In "Research Library Collection in a Changing Universe: Four Points of View," edited by Dan C. Hazen and J. Gormly Miller. *College and Research Libraries* 45: 214–24.

Harvey, John F., and Spyers-Duran, Peter. 1984. "The Effect of Inflation on Academic Libraries." In *Austerity Management in Academic Libraries,* edited by John F. Harvey and Peter Spyers-Duran. Metuchen, N.J.: Scarecrow.

Heim, Kathleen M., ed. 1983. *The Status of Women in Librarianship: Historical, Sociological, and Economic Issues.* New York: Neal-Schuman.

Henry, W.M.; Leigh, J.A.; Tedd, L.A.; and Williams, P.W. 1980. *Online Searching.* London: Butterworth & Co.

Hewitt, Joe A. July/September 1984. "Technical Services in 1983." *Library Resources and Technical Services* 28: 205–18.

Hewitt, Joe A., and Gleim, David E. March 1979. "Adopting AACR2: The Case for Not Closing the Catalog." *American Libraries* 10: 118–21.

Holicky, Bernard H. July 1984. "Collection Development vs. Resource Sharing: The View from the Small Academic Library." *Journal of Academic Librarianship* 10: 146–47.

Holley, Edward G. July 1976. "Librarians, 1876–1976." *Library Trends* 25: 177–207.

———. 1977. "What Lies Ahead for Academic Libraries?" In *Academic Libraries by the Year 2000: Essays Honoring Jerrold Orne,* edited by Herbert Poole. New York: R.R. Bowker.

———. 1984. "North American Efforts at Worldwide Acquisitions Since 1945." Unpublished paper delivered at the International Conference on Research Library Cooperation, October 1–3, 1984, Stanford, California.

Hoover, Ryan E. 1980. *The Library and Information Manager's Guide to Online Services.* White Plains, N.Y.: Knowledge Industry Publications.

Horner, S.J. May 1981. "Bravely Embracing Technology: The Clarkson College Commitment." *Wilson Library Bulletin* 55: 656–60.

Horny, Karen L. March 1982. "Online Catalogs: Coping with the Choices." *Journal of Academic Librarianship* 8: 14-19.

Janke, Richard V. September 1983. "BRS/After Dark: The Birth of Online Self-Service." *Online* 7: 12–29.

Johnson, Edward R. January 1977. "Subject Divisional Organization in American University Libraries, 1939–1974." *Library Quarterly* 47: 23–42.

Jones, C. Lee. July 1984. "Library Patrons in an Age of Discontinuity: Artifacts of Technology." *Journal of Academic Librarianship* 10: 151–54.

Kaplan, Louis. September 1973. "Participation: Some Basic Considerations on the Theme of Academe." *College and Research Libraries* 34: 235–41.

Karr, Ronald Dale. July 1984. "The Changing Profile of University Library Directors, 1966–1981." *College and Research Libraries* 45: 282–85.

Kaser, David. 1977. "The Effect of the Revolution of 1969–1970 on University Library Administration." In *Academic Libraries by the Year 2000: Essays Honoring Jerrold Orne,* edited by Herbert Poole. New York: R.R. Bowker.

———. 1980. "Collection Building in American Universities." In *University Library History: An International Review,* edited by James Thompson. New York: K.G. Saur.

Kent, Allen, et al. 1979. *Use of Library Materials: The University of Pittsburgh Study.* New York: Marcel Dekker.

Kirk, Thomas G., ed. 1984. *Increasing the Teaching Role of Academic Libraries.* New Directions for Teaching and Learning No. 18. San Francisco: Jossey-Bass.

Kochen, Manfred; Reich, Victoria; and Cohen, Lee. November 1981. "Influence of Online Bibliographic Services on Student Behavior." *Journal of the American Society for Information Science* 32: 412–20.

Kronick, David A. July 1982. "Goodbye to Farewells: Resource Sharing and Cost Sharing." *Journal of Academic Librarianship* 8: 132–36.

Lamb, Connie. April 1981. "Searching in Academia: Nearly 50 Libraries Tell What They're Doing." *Online* 5: 78–81.

Lancaster, F. Wilfrid. September 1978. "Whither Libraries, Wither Libraries?" *College and Research Libraries* 39: 345–57.

———. 1982. *Libraries and Librarians in an Age of Electronics.* Arlington, Va.: Information Resources Press.

Learmont, Carol, and Van Houten, Stephen. October 1984. "Placements and Salaries, 1983: Catching Up." *Library Journal* 109: 1805–11.

Lee, Sul H., ed. 1977. *Library Budgeting: Critical Challenges for the Future.* Ann Arbor, Mich.: The Pierian Press.

Lee, Susan A. September 1977. "Conflict and Ambiguity in the Role of the Academic Library Director." *College and Research Libraries* 38: 396–403.

Lynch, Beverly P. January 1978. "The Changing Environment of Academic Libraries." *College and Research Libraries* 39: 10–14.

———. March 1982. "Options for the 80's: New Directions in Academic and Research Libraries." *College and Research Libraries* 43: 124–29.

McAnally, Arthur M. July 1952. "Organization of College and University Libraries." *Library Trends* 1: 20–36.

———. 1971. "Status of the University Librarian in the Academic Community." In *Research Librarianship: Essays in Honor of Robert B. Downs,* edited by Jerrold Orne. New York: Bowker.

McAnally, Arthur M., and Downs, Robert B. March 1973. "The Changing Role of Directors of University Libraries." *College and Research Libraries* 34: 103–25.

Malinconico, S. Michael. September 1980. "The National Bibliographic Network: A Patrician Pursuit." *Library Journal* 105: 1791–92.

———. June 1984. "Catalogs and Cataloging: Innocent Pleasures and Enduring Controversies." *Library Journal* 109: 1210–13.

Malinconico, S. Michael, and Fasana, Paul J. 1979. *The Future of the Catalog: The Library's Choices.* White Plains, N.Y.: Knowledge Industry Publications.

Marchant, Maurice P. 1976. *Participative Management in Academic Libraries.* Westport, Conn.: Greenwood Press.

———. April 1982. "Participative Management, Job Satisfaction, and Service." *Library Journal* 107: 782–84.

Marchant, Maurice P., and Smith, Nathan. November 1982. "The Research Libraries Director's View of Library Education." *College and Research Libraries* 43: 437–44.

Markuson, Barbara Evans. March 1979. "Cooperation and Library Network Development." *College and Research Libraries* 40: 125–35.

Martell, Charles R., Jr. 1983. *The Client-Centered Academic Library: An Organizational Model.* Westport, Conn.: Greenwood Press.

Martell, Charles, and Untawale, Mercedes. January 1983. "Work Enrichment for Academic Libraries." *Journal of Academic Librarianship* 8: 339–43.

Martin, Murray S. 1981. *Issues in Personnel Management in Academic Libraries.* Greenwich, Conn.: JAI Press.

Martin, Susan K. June 1984. "The New Technologies and Library Networks." *Library Journal* 109: 1194–96.

Massman, Vergil F. 1977. "Changes that Will Affect College Library Collection Development." In *Academic Libraries by the Year 2000: Essays Honoring Jerrold Orne,* edited by Herbert Poole. New York: R.R. Bowker.

Matheson, Nina W. May 1984. "The Academic Library Nexus." *College and Research Libraries* 45: 207–13.

Matthews, Joseph R. June 1982a. "Online Public Access Catalogs: Assessing the Potential." *Library Journal* 107: 1067–71.

———. 1982b. *Public Access to Online Catalogs.* Weston, Conn.: Online, Inc.

Meadow, Charles T. July 1979a. "The Computer as a Search Intermediary." *Online* 3: 54–59.

———. January 1979b. "Online Searching and Computer Programming: Some Behavioral Similarities (or. . .Why End Users Will
Eventually Take Over the Terminal)." *Online* 3: 49–52.

Merrill-Oldham, Jan. 1984. "Preservation of Library Materials." In
The ALA Yearbook of Library and Information Services. Chicago:
American Library Association.

Metz, Paul. September 1978. "Administrative Succession in the
Academic Library." *College and Research Libraries* 39: 358–64.

———. July 1979. "The Role of the Academic Library Director."
Journal of Academic Librarianship 5: 148–52.

Michalko, James. July 1975. "Management by Objectives and the
Academic Library: A Critical Overview." *Library Quarterly* 45:
235–52.

Miller, Julia E. November 1982. "OCLC and RLIN as Reference
Tools." *Journal of Academic Librarianship* 8: 270–77.

Miller, William. 1981. "Faculty Status in the College Library." In
College Librarianship, edited by William Miller and D. Stephen
Rockwood. Metuchen, N.J.: Scarecrow.

Molyneux, Robert E., Jr. 1984. "An Examination of the Growth of
Academic Libraries in the United States, 1972/73–1981/82." Ph.D.
dissertation, University of North Carolina at Chapel Hill.

Moore, Carole Weiss. July 1981. "User Reactions to Online Catalogs:
An Exploratory Study." *College and Research Libraries* 42:
295–302.

Moran, Barbara B. September 1983. "Career Patterns of Academic
Library Administrators." *College and Research Libraries* 44:
334–44.

Munn, Robert F. January 1968. "The Bottomless Pit, or The
Academic Library As Viewed from the Administration Building."
College and Research Libraries 29: 51–54.

Munn, Robert F. January 1983. "Collection Development vs. Resource
Sharing: The Dilemma of the Middle-Level Institutions." *Journal of
Academic Librarianship* 8: 352–53.

National Enquiry into Scholarly Communication. 1979. *Scholarly
Communication: The Report of the National Enquiry.* Baltimore:
Johns Hopkins University Press.

OCLC. 1984. *Questions and Answers.* Dublin, Ohio: Online
Computer Library Center.

Ojala, Marydee. September 1982. "Using RLIN as a Reference Tool:
Ballots Revisited." *Online* 6: 24–26.

O'Neil, Robert M. 1982. "The University Administrator's View of the
University Library." In *Priorities for Academic Libraries,* edited by
Thomas J. Galvin and Beverly P. Lynch. New Directions for
Higher Education No. 39. San Francisco: Jossey-Bass.

Osburn, Charles B. 1979. *Academic Research and Library Resources.* Westport, Conn.: Greenwood Press.

———. September 1982. "Collection Development: The Link between Scholarship and Library Resources." In *Priorities for Academic Libraries,* edited by Thomas J. Galvin and Beverly P. Lynch. New Directions for Higher Education No. 39. San Francisco: Jossey-Bass.

Payne, Joyce, and Wagner, Janet. March 1984. "Librarians, Publication, and Tenure." *College and Research Libraries* 45: 133–39.

Person, Roland. March 1982. "University Undergraduate Libraries: Nearly Extinct or Continuing Examples of Evolution?" *The Journal of Academic Librarianship* 8: 4–13.

Phenix, Katharine. 1984. "Women in Librarianship." In *The ALA Yearbook of Library and Information Services.* Chicago: American Library Association.

Raffel, Jeffrey A. November 1974. "From Economic to Political Analysis of Library Decision Making." *College and Research Libraries* 35: 412–23.

Richards, Timothy F. March 1984. "The Online Catalog: Issues in Planning and Development." *Journal of Academic Librarianship* 10: 4–9.

Rogers, Rutherford D., and Weber, David C. 1971. *University Library Administration.* New York: H. W. Wilson.

Salmon, Stephen R. 1975. *Library Automation Systems.* New York: Marcel Dekker.

Sawtelle, H.A. June 1878. "The College Librarianship." *Library Journal* 3: 162.

Schmidt, C. James. 1979. "Faculty Status in Academic Libraries: Retrospective and Prospect." In *New Horizons for Academic Libraries,* edited by Robert D. Stueart and Richard D. Johnson. New York: K.G. Saur.

Sewell, Robert G. May 1983. "Faculty Status and Librarians: The Rationale and the Case of Illinois." *College and Research Libraries* 44: 212–22.

Shaw, Ward. September 1982. "Resource Sharing and the Network Approach." In *Priorities for Academic Libraries,* edited by Thomas J. Galvin and Beverly Lynch. New Directions for Higher Education No. 39. San Francisco: Jossey-Bass.

Shaw, William M., Jr. November 1978. "A Practical Journal Usage Technique." *College and Research Libraries* 39: 479–84.

Shiflett, Orvin Lee. 1981. *Origins of American Academic Librarianship.* Norwood, N.J.: Ablex Publishing Corp.

Simpson, Donald B. November 1983. "Center for Research Libraries: Meeting the Opportunity to Fulfill the Promise: A Symposium." *Journal of Academic Librarianship* 9: 258–69.

Smith, John Brewster, and Knapp, Sara D. September 1981. "Data Base Royalty Fees and the Growth of Online Search Services in Academic Libraries." *Journal of Academic Librarianship* 7: 206–12.

Sparks, David G.E. September 1980. "Academic Librarianship: Professional Strivings and Political Realities." *College and Research Libraries* 41: 408–21.

Stone, Ann. 1982. "Library Personnel Issues in the 1970s." *The Bookmark* 51 & 52: 31–53.

Stone, Elizabeth W. July 1971. "Personnel Development and Continuing Education in Libraries: Introduction." *Library Trends* 20: 3–18.

Stueart, Robert D. 1982. "The Education of Academic Librarians." In *Academic Librarianship,* edited by Robert Stueart. New York: Neal-Schuman.

———. September 1984. "Preparing Libraries for Change." *Library Journal* 109: 1724–26.

Sullivan, Daniel. March 1982. "Libraries and Liberal Arts Colleges: Tough Times in the Eighties." *College and Research Libraries* 43: 119–23.

Talbot, Richard J. September 1982. "Financing the Academic Library." In *Priorities for Academic Libraries,* edited by Thomas J. Galvin and Beverly P. Lynch. New Directions for Higher Education No. 39. San Francisco: Jossey-Bass.

——— 1984. "College and University Libraries." In *The Bowker Annual of Library and Book Trade Information,* edited by Julia Ehresmann. 29th ed. New York: R.R. Bowker.

Taylor, Merrily E. September 1984. "Participatory Management and the New Librarian Model." *Journal of Academic Librarianship* 10: 201–3.

Tucker, John Mark. 1979. "The Origins of Bibliographic Instruction in Academic Libraries, 1976–1914." In *New Horizons for Academic Libraries,* edited by Robert D. Stueart and Richard D. Johnson. New York: K.G. Saur.

Tucker, Marc S., ed. 1983–84. *Computers on Campus: Working Papers.* AAHE Current Series in Higher Education No. 2. Washington, D.C.: American Association for Higher Education. ED 240 947. 47 pp. MF–$1.19; PC–$5.49.

Veaner, Allen B. April 1984. "Librarians: The Next Generation." *Library Journal* 109: 623–25.

Wanger, Judith, and Landau, Ruth N. May 1980. "Nonbibliographic On-line Data Base Services." *Journal of the American Society for Information Science* 31: 171–80.

Weatherford, John W. 1976. *Collective Bargaining and the Academic Librarian.* Metuchen, N.J.: Scarecrow.

———. February 1980. "Collective Bargaining and the Academic Librarian: 1976–1979." *Library Journal* 105: 481–82.

Webb, William H. 1977. "Collection Development for the University and Large Research Library: More and More Versus Less and Less." In *Academic Libraries by the Year 2000: Essays Honoring Jerrold Orne,* edited by Herbert Poole. New York: R.R. Bowker.

Webster, Duane E. 1977. "Choices Facing Academic Libraries in Allocating Scarce Resources." In *Library Budgeting: Critical Challenges for the Future,* edited by Sul H. Lee. Ann Arbor, Mich.: Pierian.

Webster, Duane E., and Gardner, Jeffrey. May 1975. "Strategies for Improving the Performance of Academic Libraries." *Journal of Academic Librarianship* 1: 13–18.

White, Herbert S. March 1979. "Library Materials Prices and Academic Library Practices: Between Scylla and Charybdis." *Journal of Academic Librarianship* 5: 20–23.

Williams, Martha. 1983. "Databases, Computer Readable." In *The ALA Yearbook of Library and Information Services.* Chicago: American Library Association.

————. 1984. "Highlights of the Online Database Field—Statistics, Pricing, and New Delivery Mechanisms." In *National Online Meeting Proceedings, 1984,* edited by Martha E. Williams and Thomas H. Hogan. Medford, N.J.: Learned Information.

Wilson, Pauline. April 1979. "Librarians as Teachers: The Study of an Organization Fiction." *Library Quarterly* 49: 146–62.

Winkler, Karen J. 6 October 1982. "New Company Plans 'Electronic Journals' That Can Be Read on Computer Screens." *Chronicle of Higher Education* 24: 25–26.

ASHE-ERIC HIGHER EDUCATION RESEARCH REPORTS

Starting in 1983, the Association for the Study of Higher Education **assumed** cosponsorship of the Higher Education Research Reports with the ERIC Clearinghouse on Higher Education. For the previous 11 years, ERIC and the American Association for Higher Education prepared and published the reports.

Each report is the definitive analysis of a tough higher education problem, based on a thorough research of pertinent literature and institutional experiences. Report topics, identified by a national survey, are written by noted practitioners and scholars with prepublication manuscript reviews by experts.

Ten monographs in the ASHE-ERIC Higher Education Research Report series are published each year, available individually or by subscription. Subscription to 10 issues is $55 regular; $40 for members of AERA, AAHE, and AIR; $35 for members of ASHE. (Add $7.50 outside U.S.)

Prices for single copies, including 4th class postage and handling, are $7.50 regular and $6.00 for members of AERA, AAHE, AIR, and ASHE. If faster 1st class postage is desired for U.S. and Canadian orders, for each publication ordered add $.75; for overseas, add $4.50. For VISA and MasterCard payments, give card number, expiration date, and signature. Orders under $25 must be prepaid. Bulk discounts are available on orders of 10 or more of a single title. Order from the Publications Department, Association for the Study of Higher Education, One Dupont Circle, Suite 630, Washington, D.C. 20036, (202) 296-2597. Write for a complete list of Higher Education Research Reports and other ASHE and ERIC publications.

1982 Higher Education Research Reports

1. Rating College Teaching: Criterion Studies of Student Evaluation-of-Instruction Instruments
   Sidney E. Benton

2. Faculty Evaluation: The Use of Explicit Criteria for Promotion, Retention, and Tenure
   Neal Whitman and Elaine Weiss

3. The Enrollment Crisis: Factors, Actors, and Impacts
   J. Victor Baldridge, Frank R. Kemerer, and Kenneth C. Green

4. Improving Instruction: Issues and Alternatives for Higher Education
   Charles C. Cole, Jr.

5. Planning for Program Discontinuance: From Default to Design
   Gerlinda S. Melchiori

6. State Planning, Budgeting, and Accountability: Approaches for Higher Education
   Carol E. Floyd

7. The Process of Change in Higher Education Institutions
   Robert C. Nordvall

8. Information Systems and Technological Decisions: A Guide for Non-Technical Administrators
   Robert L. Bailey

9. Government Support for Minority Participation in Higher Education
   Kenneth C. Green

10. The Department Chair: Professional Development and Role Conflict
    David B. Booth

1983 Higher Education Research Reports

1. The Path to Excellence: Quality Assurance in Higher Education
   Laurence R. Marcus, Anita O. Leone, and Edward D. Goldberg

2. Faculty Recruitment, Retention, and Fair Employment: Obligations and Opportunities
   John S. Waggaman

3. Meeting the Challenges: Developing Faculty Careers
   Michael C. T. Brookes and Katherine L. German

4. Raising Academic Standards: A Guide to Learning Improvement
   Ruth Talbott Keimig

5. Serving Learners at a Distance: A Guide to Program Practices
   Charles E. Feasley

6. Competence, Admissions, and Articulation: Returning to the Basics in Higher Education
   Jean L. Preer

7. Public Service in Higher Education: Practices and Priorities
   Patricia H. Crosson

8. Academic Employment and Retrenchment: Judicial Review and Administrative Action
   Robert M. Hendrickson and Barbara A. Lee

9. Burnout: The New Academic Disease
   Winifred Albizu Meléndez and Rafael M. de Guzmán

10. Academic Workplace: New Demands, Hightened Tensions
    Ann E. Austin and Zelda F. Gamson

1984 Higher Education Research Reports

1. Adult Learning: State Policies and Institutional Practices
   K. Patricia Cross and Anne-Marie McCartan

2. Student Stress: Effects and Solutions
   Neal A. Whitman, David C. Spendlove, and Claire H.
   Clark

3. Part-time Faculty: Higher Education at a Crossroads
   Judith M. Gappa

4. Sex Discrimination Law in Higher Education: The Lessons of
   the Past Decade
   J. Ralph Lindgren, Patti T. Ota, Perry A. Zirkel, and Nan
   Van Gieson

5. Faculty Freedoms and Institutional Accountability: Interactions
   and Conflicts
   Steven G. Olswang and Barbara A. Lee

6. The High-Technology Connection: Academic/Industrial
   Cooperation for Economic Growth
   Lynn G. Johnson

7. Employee Educational Programs: Implications for Industry and
   Higher Education
   Suzanne W. Morse

8. Academic Libraries: The Changing Knowledge Centers of
   Colleges and Universities
   Barbara B. Moran